MW01702231

Building My Dream

A Log Cabin and a Life

John Sievel

ISBN: 978-0-9600879-2-1

johnsievel@perryhillpublishing.com

Published by:

Perry Hill Publishing
PO Box 203
Ashford, CT 06278
<www.perryhillpublishing.com>

Dedication

This book is dedicated to all those
who build their dream.
With their hands.

Disclaimer

I was living in a school bus, and building the log cabin home of my dreams. It was one of the most intense times of my life, and I want to share it as honestly as I can. But it should not be construed, by any means, as fact. Some of the events and people described may seem fictitious, and perhaps they are. However, often fact is stranger than fiction. I'll just leave it at that.

Consider the characters portrayed here as fictitious. Any correspondence to actual persons, alive or dead, is purely coincidental. All names used here are fictitious, in a desire to protect the privacy of the innocent, and perhaps the guilty as well.

TABLE OF CONTENTS

The Dream

That's all I ever wanted. To be in the woods, and dig in the dirt. To have intercourse with the land. To be deeply, playfully enmeshed in my environment, and have it infused into me. To care for the environment, and enjoy its many gifts. To play and work in the forest, and harvest its water, wood, and clean air. To enrich the soil and be nourished by its gifts of food and drink. And to put my back into my living, giving my labor, and receiving muscles, health, and food.

I would be living in a log cabin on a hill, built of trees from the forest, with a large vegetable garden growing nearby. The house would honestly show what it is made of, never hiding anything behind a fake veneer. It would be oriented south, to be partially heated by the sun, and large windows on that side would provide stunning views. The electricity and hot water would come from the sun. A woodstove would provide heat while it cooked my dinner.

And I would build it myself, with my own strong hands and willing back. And live a life of pleasure, health and meaning.

Homework

Dreaming is nice, but eventually, you do wake up. At this point you begin to prepare to actualize the dream, to make it real. To acquire the knowledge and learn the skills that will enable the transformation of a dream into reality.

For me, the process began when I was a child. I was very fortunate to learn so many basic skills from my father Stanley, who built our family's home in the 1950s. Not only did he teach me the basic skills of carpentry, masonry, plumbing, and metal working, but he instilled in me the knowledge that it was actually possible to build your own home.

As I grew up, I was drawn to books that illuminated a path toward building not only a home, but also a lifestyle that would make the dream a reality. Perhaps the book that most influenced me was The Owner Built Home, by Ken Kern. The book exposed me to so many new, unconventional ways of building and thinking about building. The companion book, The Owner-Built Homestead, by Barbara and Ken Kern, centered the home itself within the broader framework of a working farm, which would not only provide shelter, but food and health.

Ken's books were written in the 70s, and it was a different time. It was the age of Aquarius, the time of Woodstock. Opposition to the war in Vietnam had sparked a rebellion against the values and methods of the larger culture. Ken's books reflect that alternative spirit, so they appealed to me. I was not just interested in building a house, I wanted to build a life, too.

A major feature of the dominant culture was, and still is, its insatiable thirst for fossil fuel. Many of us understood, then, that the this was driving world events in a very negative way. The United States could no longer meet its enormous demand for oil domestically, so this led to the overthrow of a legitimately elected government in Iran to ensure a supply. When OPEC (Organization of Oil Exporting Nations) initiated the oil embargo of 1973, the entire US economy was affected. Gasoline was rationed, and it was only possible to buy every other day, depending on the last letter or number of your license plate.

And then there was the filth that fossil fuels belched into the environment. Back in those days, you could not see more than a block down New York City streets, the pollution was so thick. In 1969, an oil slick on the surface of the Cayuga River caught fire. Acid rain had already killed most of the trees in the high Appalachian Mountains in the southeast United States. Back in the 1970s, there was some awareness that the burning of fossil fuel was beginning to destabilize the environment, but this was very much an alternative view. But for me, the filth and destabilization of the world was more than enough to avoid using fossil fuels in any way I could.

A local organization which still exists, Peoples Actions for Clean Energy (PACE) was hugely influential for me. I cannot overstate how important the house tours that the group ran were. New homes were featured that utilized solar gain through large, south facing windows for heating. The homes demonstrated the enormous benefits to be gained by simply orienting the house correctly, and building in heat storage. I still remember visiting one of the houses on a sunny, cold day. There was a foot of snow on the ground, but the driveway was clear. The home's owner, a professional architect, had designed and positioned it to make use of the wind to automatically clear the driveway. The interior was toasty on a cold day, without using any fuel at all. That is what I was after: knowing about, understanding, and using the natural world's gifts as much as possible.

I also took some courses that taught me new skills that would prove very helpful. One nonprofit, the Connecticut Housing Investment Fund (CHIF) had a goal of helping residents of the state that might have limited financial means build their own home. The course met two nights per week for a classroom phase, with required reading. And there was a hands-on portion on Saturday mornings, in an unheated warehouse.

Even though I had previous experience with building techniques, I found the Saturday workshops very valuable. Each Saturday focused on a different topic, from foundations, framing, sheathing, roofing, sheetrock, plumbing, electrical, finish carpentry, and windows and doors. I was pleasantly surprised by how patient and empathetic the instructors were. After all, they were professional tradesmen, so teaching secrets of their trade to us was more than generous.

I really appreciated the sense of humor displayed by many of the instructors. I remember one instructor reaching into his pouch to pick up a nail, which came into his hand with its head down. He looked at it, and then tossed it aside. "They put the head on the wrong end," he explained. It did illustrate how much time can be consumed simply by flipping half of the nails around. But nowadays, with nail guns consuming a belt of nails like a machine gun, all the nails come in with their heads up.

Nails. I learned a lot about nails. You use a lot of nails to hold a wood house together, and they are very important to assure its overall strength. It turns out that you can increase the strength of a wood house significantly at very little additional cost by using galvanized nails instead of bright, uncoated nails. Galvanized nails are coated with zinc, which makes them much more corrosion resistant. It also makes them adhere to the wood much better, making a much stronger joint. And if you use nails with rings around the shank, the connection to the wood will be even better.

In terms of the total cost of the house, premium nails add almost no additional cost, but a lot of extra strength. Something to think about as hurricanes are becoming more powerful. A very good idea, until you have to pull a nail out. Of course, that would never happen to me.

Most of the instructors completely understood the financial situation of many of the students. I remember one instructor explaining how a cut off plastic soda bottle with some holes punched in it could be used as a cap on a pipe to drain excess water from a cellar window well. A lot cheaper than buying the factory-made covers, and they are recycled!

But they also imparted a sense of how hard the work is. We were told that no matter how good shape you think you are in, you will be awakening new muscles you never knew you had. That proved to be so true. It gave us a real sense of what we were up against.

Another course that proved very valuable was a solar energy course that was taught at the Harford Graduate Center. Solar energy was a new and up-and-coming technology, and I wanted to understand it. The course was designed for engineers, and covered the ins and outs of gathering, storing, and moving solar energy.

A key concept is the idea of using a massive substance like concrete to store heat that is gathered during a sunny day, to be released at night. This is something that I remembered later, when I began considering building a log cabin. The heavy oak is not that good of an insulator, but it does store a lot of heat. As I discovered, this really does help keep the house warm, particularly in the spring and the fall when there is significant solar gain.

Another lesson that proved to be especially useful to me was how to design a thermosiphon hot water heating system. The basic idea is to use gravity, instead of pumps, to move hot water. Since hot water is less dense than cold water, it will rise in a pipe. My hot water system positions the solar collectors below the tank. There is no need for a pump to move the water, or electricity to run it, or a controller for a pump, or even a check valve. The only moving part is water, and the power to move it comes from the sun, aided by earth's gravity.

Can you imagine a simpler, cheaper, more reliable, more elegant solution? And wow, does it work well, as I found out years later. The sun and the earth's gravity have been reliably providing most of my hot water for many years.

So, learn your lessons well

Bricks

There they were, piled high, and surrounded by charred wood and mostly melted metal. It was the site of the former Shaboo Inn, a beloved local nightclub and concert venue in the 1970's. The bricks had absorbed the sounds of B.B. King, Aerosmith, and Count Basie's band. I wanted those bricks.

My infatuation with bricks began in childhood. One of my most beloved toys was a large canister of plastic bricks. On the front was the rendering of a boy crouching like a giant before the building he had created. I kept adding to the set every Christmas, until I could build my own little city.

I looked at the huge heap of tangled bricks. I wanted them. But what would I do with them? At that point I did not even own land. I walked over to the man directing a huge front-end loader.

"What are you doing with the bricks?" I asked.

The reply: "They're for sale, ten cents apiece. Of course, you have to clean them."

I looked at the heap. Every once in a while, there was a single brick, still encrusted in mortar. But more often, it was 2, 3, 4 or more stuck together, sometimes whole chunks of wall.

Some were from the bathrooms that I remembered were painted blue inside. They were not even separate bricks.

"How do you count them?" I asked.

"It's around 5000 in a full load, for $500," he replied.

I did a quick calculation. Well, it seemed like a lot of bricks for $500. And they were wonderful bricks, water struck, hand-made, and at least one hundred years old. And the vibes of B.B. King? How could I resist. I made an impulse purchase.

"I'll take a load," I said.

But then, where exactly would they take them to? As of yet, I did not own a patch of ground to put them on. I had to get permission from the owner of the house we were renting. Amazingly, she said yes.

On the designated delivery day as I waited, I noticed my neighbor Hank working across the street. Finally, the massive 14-wheeler dump truck heaped with bricks stopped in front of the house. As it backed into the driveway, Hank came running over.

"Stop," he yelled. "What are you doing with those bricks?"

I had a plan. The truck would back down the driveway, and then back off to the side of the yard, and drop the load there, in a semi-hidden area. But Hank objected vigorously. It would be near his property line. He was already in trouble with the town for running an unauthorized junk business, and didn't want the hassle.

"No," he shouted. "You can't do that. They will think they're mine. Put them behind the house instead."

I had to admit, there was merit to the idea. It would be completely hidden there, and I could "clean" them undisturbed.

But there was one problem. The truck would have to cross over the pipe to the septic system. As it backed slowly down the driveway, I studied the asphalt with fascination as it bent under the enormous weight. But the truck rolled slowly over the stressed pipe, and at least it did not collapse into a hole. The truck had no trouble dumping the load behind the house and retreating, once it was much lighter. And the toilet still flushed.

I walked behind the house and gazed up at the mountain of construction debris. What had I done?

Cleaning bricks became my hobby for the next two years. But it had nothing to do with "cleaning". It had more to do with chiseling bricks out of construction debris. I armed myself with a large chisel, called a Brick Set, a hammer, and a stool at the base of my mountain.

The procedure was a bit repetitive. First, find a chunk of wall to break apart. Often there were pieces of two or three bricks stuck together in various ways. Usually, I could smash them apart by pounding the Brick Set into the mortar joints.

Then I would peel the mortar off the individual bricks. Sometimes it was soft and flaked off easily. Sometimes it was so hard I had to scrape it off with the Brick Set and a hammer. Sometimes the brick broke. Sometimes I gave up.

Slowly, over the course of days, weeks, months, years, I produced several stacks of actual antique bricks on pallets. It was painstakingly slow, but the bricks I produced were gems: hand-made, water struck, 100-year-old masterpieces, each one different. Some had the fingerprints of the child laborer that made them. I set those aside in a separate pile.

But that load contained more than bricks. Once I cleaned the mortar off, it accumulated into its own mini-mountain that I would need to remove. Years later, I found that it was a good material to pave our driveway with, once I removed the broken glass. And there were a couple of heavy cast-iron doors. I knew that I would find a use for all of it someday. It was a part of my future now.

Oh, What a Tangled Web We Weave

The story really started with Olivia, in 1975. I was a software engineer employed by the Infant Studies Lab at the University of Connecticut, where she was a graduate student working on a PhD. She grabbed my attention like no woman ever had before. She was tall, lean, strong and sassy. And then there was the boots. Big Frye boots that she did not hesitate to stomp around in. Them boots was made for walking...

She loved animals, and soon had a menagerie to add to the dog and cat she brought from New York City. One spare room contained a turtle and two parrots. The box trained (more or less) rabbit just hopped around the house, chewing up the telephone wires. The cat was fond of peeing in guest's shoes that she didn't like. The Wookie (guinea pig) lived outside. And so on. And then there was the horse, not living in the house, thank God. Shom really was the love of her life. Oh, how she loved feeling him between her legs.

Soon after I met Olivia, she told me about her girlfriend Hannah, in Vermont. Hannah was building a log cabin on a piece of land she bought. Olivia would make the 4-hour drive to Vermont to spend weekends with Hannah. I was curious.

Olivia and I planned to hike part of the Appalachian Trail

in Vermont, and end by visiting Hannah. I had never done any overnight trail hiking before, but she had. Growing up in Colorado, she had been on many "forced marches" through the mountains that she loved with her father. She helped me select a down sleeping bag that kept me warm for many years, and an external frame back pack that travelled many miles with me since.

The section that we chose, from Rutland to Woodstock, is known as the inter-mountain section, between the Green Mountains of Vermont and the White Mountains of New Hampshire. The trail crosses the mountains ridges from West to East. The mountains are not particularly tall, but there is a lot of up and down.

We spent our first night at the Stoney Brook Shelter. There was no one else there, so we enjoyed frolicking naked in the icy brook. It was all new to me, and absolutely delightful.

But the next couple of days did wear on us. The heat, the constant up and down. The joy was gone. When we finally emerged near Woodstock, the thermometer registered a full 100 degrees!

We were not happy campers. The thrill was gone. We hitch hiked back to the car individually, not wanting to be with each other just then. It was the first and last time we ever hiked together, though I continued hiking for many years.

The drive to Hannah's brightened our mood considerably. As we drove up her long driveway, I was astonished. A hand-built log cabin was sitting on a hand-built stone foundation. Hannah was hauling rocks up a scaffold to build the stone fireplace. On either side of it, two hand-made stained-glass windows illuminated the scene in red and blue.

She came down the ladder to meet me. It was the only time I ever saw Hannah stop working to greet me. She was short, solid, and sun tanned. And never stopped moving. She was a volcano, energy and heat pouring out of her. I did not understand it then, but only later did I come to realize how any one person could accomplish what she did. She worked all the time. Almost.

I was hooked by what she was doing. It became a regular thing for me, those four-hour drives to Vermont. I learned how to handle a chainsaw, and plant carrots. I helped her, and she taught me. A lot.

On one trip in the winter, the temperature dropped to minus 15°F. It was so cold that the bindings on my cross-country skis shattered when I tried to put them on. They had been riding on a rack on the roof of the car. That did make it difficult, slogging the half-mile up Hannah's unplowed driveway in two feet of snow. But it was an adventure, and I was young. And Hannah's wood heated cabin was warm and cozy. That was something that I would take with me, to become part of my dream.

My favorite time at Hannah's was Wood Weekend. It was always around Columbus Day, which was a legal holiday in most of New England in early October. The idea was that a lot of friends would get together, and cut, split, and stack the 10 cords of wood that Hannah needed to get through the winter.

Friends of every persuasion converged on Hannah's mountain, from city and country. We worked hard during the day. But boy, did we party at night. And eat. And drink. And smoke.

I remember one time when some friends from New York City decided they would heat up a can of baked beans in the campfire. Without opening it. About half an hour after it had been forgotten, it exploded. In a flash, the campfire was gone in a geyser and then shower of sparks. The baked beans vaporized, forming a thin, sticky film over us all. But we survived.

So now you have some idea of the quirky people that would become part of my story, my life, and my dream. The tendrils of our lives began to wrap tightly around each other

The Land

So, I had my dreams, and done my homework. I even had my bricks. Now all we needed was a place to build it. We needed land. Olivia and I had been thinking of buying a piece of land together for quite some time. Easier said than done. I had almost no savings, even though I had been trying. I was good at dreaming, and smoking pot back in those days, but not as good at working toward a goal. And Olivia was in the middle of working on a PhD.

Where would it be? On long bike rides from the University of Connecticut through the undulating folds of northeast Connecticut, I fell in love with its quiet woods, quaint farms, and verdant fields. I liked the mix of down-to-earth "Swamp Yankees", and university people, too. It was the Quiet Corner of Connecticut, the last dark area between Boston and Washington on satellite pictures. That's where we wanted our land to be. And it would be a short commute to the University of Connecticut, so Oliva could continue her studies, and I could continue working at a job I loved. But how could we make it happen?

As sometimes happens in life, doors can suddenly open. And when it does happen, you better be ready to walk through them. Hannah had decided to leave her owner-built homestead in Vermont and move to Connecticut. She was finding it increasingly difficult to sustain her cabinet making business in her impoverished corner of Vermont. And she was tired of the isolation of Vermont, and wanted to join her friends in Connecticut.

Olivia and I had been thinking of buying land together for a long time. Olivia needed a place to stable her horse, and I needed a place to build my dream. And now with Hannah's involvement, we decided to look around, and see if we could come up with a solution for the three of us.

I wanted a mix of forest, to provide lumber and firewood, and open land to farm. Hannah had no interest in building a house again. She also wanted to be close to the road this time, and was not interested in dealing with a long driveway. Olivia wanted to be near trails to ride her horse, and a pasture and barn to keep him in. I was not afraid of living up a long driveway, since I would be providing my own solar electricity, and would not need a connection to the grid. I could consider cheaper land well removed from a road and a power line. We all wanted a piece of beautiful, rural land to live and work on.

Olivia was focused on finishing her PhD work, so Hannah and I decided to spend some time land shopping. We contacted several agents, and began scanning the advertisements. We were careful to describe what we were looking for. Maybe something like an old farm with a house and barn near the road, and some undeveloped back land for Olivia and me. But over and over again, we wasted time being shown completely inappropriate land, often a five-acre lot in a subdivision with a ranch house on it.

Finally, we connected with an agent that knew exactly what we were looking for. And miracle of miracles, he had almost the perfect piece, the first property he showed us. It was an old farm, with two pastures near the road, and a large back area that was wooded, and included the top of a hill. The old farmhouse had long since vanished, but the site was easy to build on and accessible. It had not been farmed since the 1930s, so the soil and water were clean, free of agricultural chemicals. There was plenty of frontage on the road, so it would be possible to subdivide off several lots to sell.

The land had one other huge advantage. It had an option for owner financing. The owner was willing to hold a mortgage on the land. We would pay him his down payment, and then make the monthly payments until we totally owned it.

It was listed as 52 1/2 acres, plus or minus. Turns out the plus and minus signs were quite common in land listings in New England. They usually meant "more or less". Large pieces of land had not been surveyed in a long time, usually since the mid-1800s. That's when all the surveyors left New England to go work in the promised land of the Midwest. When we asked the agent to show us the boundaries of the land, he laughed, and rather matter of factly said, "I can't do that." He did show us the two utility poles along the road that marked the front corners, but that is as far is he would go. So, we were interested in a piece of land, but we didn't really know how big it was, or even exactly where it was. Nice.

The first suggestion he gave us was to talk to the neighbors to get some of the oral history of the place. We contacted two old-time neighbors along one side, and they both agreed that the land had always gone between the two utility poles the agent had shown us. And they both agreed that the land included the top of the hill. At least it was a start.

We asked for permission to walk around the land on our own, and that was granted. Olivia and I started marching through the woods, back and forth to the top of the hill looking for stone walls and barbed wire. We found a lot of both. Very confusing.

We knew the next step was to go to the town hall, and start looking at the land records, but we had no idea just how difficult and time-consuming that would be.

And so, Olivia and I started our journey into the past. For four afternoons a week, we submerged ourselves into the vault at the town hall. We easily found a record for our piece of land. But when we looked for any sort of descriptions of markings on the land, there were none. Instead, what we found were the names of the owners who abutted the land on each side.

We decided we needed to go back to the previous owner, to see if we could find a better description. We followed the link back to the volume and page for that owner. Unfortunately, we found the same thing again. It was always some form of: "bounded on the East by so-and-so, or the heirs of so-and-so, bounded on the South by who knows who, or the heirs of who knows who..."

And so it went. Year after year, decade after decade, century after century. It did get interesting as we sank back deeper in time. The records were hand written in beautiful, nearly illegible script. And they were written on parchment, made from sheep skins.

We learned things we never expected to, such as the fact that we would not own the mineral rights to whatever existed under our land, since it had been sold separately a hundred years earlier. This did not particularly concern us, since we were not inclined to drill for oil anytime soon. And we learned that one of the transactions included one cow, fourteen hens, 32 chickens, and farm tools. Another required the new owner to drive the previous owner's mother to church every Sunday for the rest of her life. Interesting, but really, not very helpful.

And I am radically simplifying, too. Our land was not always a single piece. No, over time, parts of it had been broken off and owned by neighbors, and then recombined in new, very creative ways. It was like some sort of jigsaw puzzle that kept morphing over time, the irregular pieces breaking apart and recombining in almost unimaginable ways.

After around a month of digging down into the deep, dark, past, we began to hit pay dirt. On two of those sub-pieces that would eventually become our land, we found some sort of measurements. They were of the form: "10 chains and 5 links 93 degrees North, ...". Wow, what was this?

A colleague I worked with who grew up in England was familiar with the dimensions, which likely migrated across the Atlantic with the Pilgrims. We learned that a chain contained 66 feet, and was composed of 100 links. So at least now we could convert to feet.

And what about the compass headings? We did not know that the magnetic North Pole has been wandering around significantly in the last several hundred years, our interval of interest. But at least now we had a rough idea of the boundaries of part of our land.

After careful study we concluded that in the 1830s or so, Mr. Ralph Bigbee divided his land roughly into thirds, and gave each of his three sons a piece. We could see that there were clear records of transfers for the outer two pieces going forward to modern times. For the middle piece: nothing. We could not find any place where that piece was transferred.

But there was one clue. We did find a record of marriage of the son owning the middle piece to a woman from St. Johnsbury Vermont. I had been planning a trip to northern Vermont to hike the Long Trail to Canada. I decided I would drop by the town hall in St Johnsbury afterwards to see if I could find a will.

My hike went well, and when I arrived at the town hall, they were very gracious to smelly me. After I paid the $2 fee, I held a copy of the will of the previous owner in my hands, but it made no mention of the land in Connecticut. The land had simply been abandoned.

Now the mystery of that plus and minus started coming into focus. We knew that if the road frontage was as people said, the land could not include the top of the hill and still be 52 1/2 acres. It would have to be more. And we also knew that the eastern side piece did go back to the top of the hill, since we now had a real measurement for that. So, it seemed likely that we were looking at more than 52 1/2 acres.

Now that we were pretty sure the top of the hill was included, I wanted to go for it. But it was quite a large financial commitment, so we decided to invite in other friends as partners. We got no takers. It was not a sure thing. And since we really did not know where it was, it was a tough sell.

We decided to proceed on our own. We made a first offer that was refused. But our second offer of $52,000 was accepted. It was stunning! Suddenly, we were landowners, and stewards of a large piece of land, although we did not know exactly how large or exactly where it was.

When the real estate agent congratulated us on our new purchase, his comment will be long remembered by us all. "Oh, what a tangled web we weave," was his comment. And it was. We worked out a complicated agreement that covered the future subdivision of the land, as well as the down payment and monthly payment amounts.

Before long, we did solidify our investment by hiring a surveyor to actually put some pins in the ground. And we also hired an attorney to settle the little matter of the abandoned land in the middle. But when it was all over, we were the proud, clear owners of 80 acres of excellent land.

Jack

The first time I saw him, at Hannah's land in Vermont, he was making soup in a hubcap over a blow torch. He was living in his truck, so this was just his kitchen. He seemed to have an affinity for me, probably because I lived in a school bus, and shit in the woods. One of the "savages", as he called us feral people.

His truck was stuffed to the windows with Boston Globes. "Good insulation," he would say. He always knew what was going on in the world, long before there was an Internet.

He was not tall or big but he was strong and wiry. He looked much younger than his 50 years, but his walk was stiff, impeded by too many years of too much hard work. His face was tanned and bearded, his eyes green and piercing. Always, he wore warn work boots, cheap jeans that didn't fit well, layers of flannel shirts, and a tractor themed baseball cap. The number of layers of shirts varied with the season, but the look was always the same.

Over the years, Jack and I spent quite a bit of time in the cab of his old flatbed truck, hauling logs or lumber. He told stories of his youth in the Boston suburbs. His mother was a school teacher, so that's probably what infected him with the reading bug. Then he had a nice dairy farm in Vermont, and two daughters there. But things did not work out, so he was living in his truck.

Soon after we bought the land, we hired Jack to log it. He would use a small tractor, doing far less damage to the forest than a big skidder. He parked his truck at the edge of the field, and he was home.

I worked with him a lot at that time, so I had ample opportunity to learn from him. How to put a chain on a log and drag it safely. How to sharpen a chainsaw for rip or crosscut. Know the species of trees, whether they were in leaf or not. And engines, tractors, all of that. He was always patient and generous with his time and knowledge.

Jack seemed to feel the pain of others more deeply than most. It was as if the volume on his empathy control was turned way up. Maybe his drinking had something to do with that. He only drank once every two weeks or so, but boy, did he drink. Peppermint schnapps or blackberry brandy.

He never drank at work. Sometimes, when he encountered "a humongous widow maker tree", he would say that he would need to have a drink before he had the courage to cut it. Of course, we both knew that he was kidding. No, he liked to sit in his truck on a beautiful afternoon, thoroughly enjoying the day while he drank.

There are so many "Jack" stories. Olivia told me that one time she was with Jack in the flatbed, hauling some logs up the steep Waterfall Road. The engine died and the brakes were not strong enough to prevent the truck from rolling down the hill backwards. Olivia had to jump out of the creeping truck and plop the wood block that was behind her seat in back of the truck tire. It was not her first trip in the flatbed, which she knew how to drive, including shifting through all ten gears.

Once the truck was stable in the middle of the road, Jack opened up the shroud and went right to work on the fuel pump. He patched the diaphragm in its heart with tin foil from a cigarette pack. She started right up.

One time, on my way back to Fort NASDAQ (more on that later), the back of the driver's seat suddenly broke. I drove the rest of the way relying on my best posture, back straighter than it's ever been. After I got to the fort, I grabbed a big stack of computer printouts and propped it up.

When I got back and showed it to Jack, he laughed. "What did you do, jerk off and break it?" he laughed. It was a plausible accusation, but I'm sure it was just my increasing bulk and tendency to lean way back that did it in. After all, it was a dainty Honda Civic seat, and I was a growing 203-pound lumberjack. All of that heavy lifting had for sure beefed me up.

But it was no problem. He would weld it in whatever position I wanted. I adjusted the seat for the last time, and Jack made it permanent with his torch. We snuffed out the smoldering seat with snow. The seat never broke again.

In general, the Honda was pretty reliable, but she did have some annoying habits. If conditions were just so, she would overheat and kind of catch fire. Usually, it happened when the air was saturated with moisture, foggy, damp. Of course, she would not run very well during one of these episodes, so I would just pull over, and put out the fire using the fire extinguisher behind the seat. After a while, I could just continue on my way with no problem.

Jack tried to figure it out, but he was stumped. He would need to bring in a consultant, "Genius Albert." So, we drove to his old apartment house in the Boston suburbs. Albert met us in the driveway, and had me run the engine at various speeds as he listened. Albert is legally blind. He quickly located the problem. He could hear a whistle we could not. He found the vacuum leak with his finger. We easily patched it.

He invited us to climb the two flights to his apartment. We followed him through a narrow canyon, with layers of "equipment" on either side. He probably had spare parts in there to fix anything. And, of course, he would know how. He fried some hotdogs in baking soda for us for lunch. He said the baking soda neutralized the acid. And I never had a problem with the Honda after that.

My favorite time working with Jack was when he stopped for a cigarette break. We would sit on a log in the middle of a ferny glen, inhaling fresh air, pungent sawdust, chainsaw fumes and cigarette smoke. He would point out a bird or a particular tree that caught his interest. Or talk about life, love, or sex.

Jack thought about sex quite a bit, and talked about it quite a bit too. He frowned on masturbation. "It's wasted," he would say. He didn't mean spilled cum. He meant that someone else could be enjoying it, too. It would be wasted.

He was not at all prejudiced against women that were less than attractive. Fat didn't matter to him. But if he felt wronged by a girlfriend, he would nominate her to receive the "hollow log" award. He would prefer the hollow log.

He was fascinated by homosexuality. Though it was not for him, it was ok by him. He just thought it would be harder for me. I told him it would be harder pretending to be straight. He understood.

One of my enduring memories is sharing a sharp, clear October evening together, sitting next to him in his truck, as a slightly smudged universe slowly swirled just outside his windshield, and we shared his bottle of peppermint schnapps. I don't remember what we talked about, but I do remember feeling intensely happy, sitting on my land, under the stars, with Jack.

Jack

Christine Acebo, Copyright 2024

Working On the Land

And so, everything changed, just like that. Suddenly, we owned the land. It made me feel the way I felt when I graduated from engineering school. Suddenly, I was an engineer. But how could it be? Just yesterday, I was not an engineer, and then, the next day, like magic, I was. It was like that with the land. Now, we were the stewards of the land. Everything about it, pretty much, was up to us. It was a little overwhelming.

On the other hand, I could not wait to get going. Olivia and I had been marching over the land for several months. Now, finally, I could start doing something with it. I knew my dream would be situated at the top of the hill. First step was to be able to get up there.

The hill is actually a drumlin: an elongated dome left behind by the glacier. The northern slope was the least steep, but the south slope dropped off quickly. That was fortunate, since we would be accessing the land from the road on the north side. Our driveway, though it would be long, would not be too steep. As Jack told us, it was good, practical land, not too difficult to build on.

I had been exploring possible routes for our driveway while we walked the land, even before we bought it. So, I knew that the shortest path from the road to the top of the hill would start on the driveway of the old homestead that had existed before. It ran up along a row of large, old, white pines between the two pastures, past the site of the old farm house and barn, which of course were long gone.

After that, there was an old road that went up into the woods, toward the top of the hill. It ended around 1000 feet up the hill, at a large rock, at the remnants of an old deer blind. It made complete sense to use it to get me part way up the hill. No trees would need to be removed.

Above the deer blind, there was nothing, just woods. But I noticed that there was a slight rise in the land that continued on to the top of the hill. It was not really a ridge, just a rise. But I decided I would try to place our driveway as close to the top of it as possible. That way, I would minimize water flowing across it.

After much walking back and forth, I laid out and flagged the route. I avoided any large trees or boulders, which were numerous. I also avoided dips or bumps in the land.

So, on the first weekend that we owned the land, I drove my Honda Civic up through the edge of the pasture, to its top. The road was too rough for my rather tiny car to continue further. Then I carried my saw, fuel, and oil up to the end of the road.

I went to work, felling trees that were in the way. At first, it felt weird, like I was stealing wood from someone else's land. But I got used to it fast. And I knew I could use the wood I cut as firewood, so I cut it into 4-foot lengths.

As I progressed further and further up the hill, it was more and more work to haul my equipment up there. Olivia had a cute, old, red VW Beetle that was not road worthy. She loaned it to the effort. Since it had good ground clearance, I found that I could drive it up the rough road, and then through the woods, right to the top of the hill. I had to be careful, though. It did not really have a floor under the driver's side. I had previously fallen through. That's why it was not road worthy, among other reasons. But it was a huge help. I loaded it up with the saw, gas, oil, tools, food, and usually a gallon of apple cider, for a day's work on the land. I kept the cider, from a local mill, in a small spring on the land to keep it cool.

Since the hill was a drumlin, the top is not exactly flat, but has a gentle curve. The slope up there is more gradual than the sides. I later learned that the top of drumlins always had been considered prime farm land in the past. So, it was not too surprising that an old stone wall partially enclosed the top of the hill. It had likely been used as a sheep pasture long ago, or maybe even as a field to grow corn.

The future house site that we selected was in one corner of the stone wall. I did not want to disturb the land that I could use in the future to grow things on. There was a gap in the wall, not far from the site. That's where our driveway would go. As I approached the top of the hill, I designed the driveway to turn left, and then right, to get it through the opening. The grade was pretty easy up there, so I knew it was a good path.

Once I had the driveway path cleared, I started on the house site. I knew that we would be relying on solar energy for heat and electricity, so I cleared a small patch to the south. I also needed a patch for the future septic system, which I cleared toward the east side of the hill, away from the future garden.

Those were good days, working on the land. It was plenty of exercise, and I was starting my dream. But very soon, I had to concentrate on making some money. After all, I had land payments to make now. So, work was limited mostly to weekends.

In the mean-time, Hannah was starting on her project. Though she had not planned on building another house, she soon accepted the idea. She planned on building a small structure which would be her cabinet making shop on the ground floor, with a loft above, where she would live. She selected a flat spot along our driveway, about 600 feet from the road. We would share the same driveway. Unlike me, she wanted grid electricity, and had to pay for the 3 poles that were needed to bring it in.

Hannah was even more eager to get going on her project than I was. She was renting a house and shop space elsewhere, and wanted to get out from that as soon as possible. The location she chose for her shop was unquestionably on the land we bought. For me, at the top of the hill, it still was not so clear. I could not start building yet.

Hannah hired a local farmer and contractor to bulldoze the driveway I laid out, up to her future shop. Then, he trucked in many loads of bank run gravel to spread on it. Bank run gravel is a mixture of rocks, gravel, sand, and a little clay, that the glacier left behind. He spread a 4 to 6-inch layer, so that the driveway would be passable, even when wet. It was amazing, the first time I drove up that driveway. It was a good start to my own driveway, too.

One time when I dropped by to visit, Hannah was in the middle of pouring concrete into the forms that would become the piers of her foundation. The huge concrete truck could not get close enough to one end because it was blocked by a load of large, 8" X 8" beams. With the concrete hardening in the truck, it fell to Jack and I to try to move them out of the way. We did manage to do that, but it was not easy. They were very heavy.

Around that time, another door unexpectedly opened for us. A friend, Joe, owned a school bus that he had converted into a camper. He would be moving to Key West, and needed someplace to park his bus while he was gone. Hannah needed a place to live. Two and two got put together, and we decided the bus would get parked on Hannah's construction site, and she would live in it while her shop was getting built.

So, that's what happened. Jack drove the bus to the land, and parked it near the last power pole, which would bring power to her shop. And she moved into the bus. As it got colder, she plugged the bus's cord into the temporary power outlet by her shop site. Then she was able to plug her electric blanket in, and be toasty warm at night.

Hannah hired Jack to help with her construction. They

erected a heavy timber frame of the 8" X 8" posts and beams, 24 feet square, on top of the concrete piers. Jack used his antique boom truck to move the heavy posts and beams. The posts were 12 feet apart, and the beams were 12 feet long. There was a single post in the middle of Hannah's first floor, which supported the beams for the second floor. They also built a small room attached to the east side, which would become Hannah's spray room. She wanted a separate room where she would apply finish to her cabinets without contaminating them with sawdust.

For the walls, they nailed 2" X 8" planks horizontally to the posts, spaced 2 feet apart vertically, around the perimeter. Hannah nailed pine boards vertically to the planks, to form the walls, in the style of a traditional post and beam barn. Then she applied a layer of 2"-inch thick Styrofoam to the outside, and built another wall of vertical pine boards outside of that. She cut some small holes in the walls, and installed barn sash in them for windows. Then she hermetically sealed them with a layer of plastic film stretched tight over them. She never liked to be cold.

They built the second floor, like the first, of 2" X 8" joists on 16-inch centers, and covered it with plywood. The roof was a Dutch Gambrel style, which would give Hannah enough space to live under. A minimal shower, with a propane tankless water heater, was installed under the stairs to the second floor. I was certainly grateful for that in the 2 years that followed. Then Hannah built a minimal kitchen on the second floor, with running hot and cold water. There was no toilet. She made do with an outhouse in the back yard, which was more than I had, going forward.

Hannah's construction style and materials influenced me a lot. I would use many of the ideas and materials in the construction of my own dream. For me, it was a good learning experience.

Hannah's shop was not the only thing going on in those days. I finished clearing the path for our long driveway. Once I saved enough money from my job to have it built, I was eager to get that done. I hired the same contractor that she used.

He bulldozed the path, and then hauled load after load of bank run gravel to spread on it. I think it was around 50 loads! A friend who lived by the route the trucks used said people were wondering what in the world was being built to require so much gravel. It was a very long driveway, nearly half a mile.

People did not usually consider anything that long to be practical. Just imagine the cost of bringing the power poles that distance. When I checked with the power company, the cost was estimated to be at least $18,000! Of course, that was impractical. I could never afford that. But we would not need a grid connection. we would produce our own solar power. The long driveway would let us live on top of the hill, deep in the middle of the woods. It was my dream. So, 50 loads of gravel.

Wow, did I enjoy those 50 loads of gravel! Finally, I could actually drive up to our house site in my Honda. I no longer needed to rely on Olivia's floorless beetle.

But it wasn't all work up there, on top of the hill. Even before the driveway got built, we did spend time camping up there. I remember one time, during black fly season. We had set up our tents in the middle of the house site clearing. But Brandy, Olivia's 100-pound German Shepard, did not at all like the flies. So, she just pushed her way right through the screen door of the tent, while it was zipped closed. It was never the same again.

We did enjoy some campfires up there, often relaxing with a drink or several, and a smoke or two. On one occasion, perhaps, a bit excessively. A friend joined us, but was not set up to camp. So, as the fire died to embers, he decided to stagger down the hill, without a flashlight, on the very dark night. I was a bit concerned, so I grabbed a light and poked my way down the hill. When I got to the bottom, I saw his big boots protruding from the side door of his van, with him sound asleep inside.

I could not understand how he could have done that, especially in those conditions. So, I practiced. I found that I could indeed navigate the half mile, even sober, even with my eyes closed. I learned how to feel the grade decreasing, and to detect the edge of the gravel with my feet. And to distinguish the smell of the wet sand, as opposed to the organic forest floor. And I noticed that on a warm, humid, night, some of the mushrooms on the edge of the driveway actually glowed faintly.

It is a skill that came in handy many years later, when I got lost in the woods on the other side of the hill, on a completely dark night. I wandered around aimlessly at first, but soon began to follow my senses down-hill. I grabbed a stick with some of the glowing mushrooms, and used that to dimly illuminate obstacles that I bumped into. Eventually, I emerged onto the highway, at 5 in the morning, coated in mud.

But I was never totally lost in the woods again.

Plans

I had done my homework. I had my bricks. And now, we even had our land. It was time to get serious. Now we needed a plan. What were we going to build? We needed detailed plans that we could submit to my town's building department.

I knew that we would be building on top of the hill. The house would be surrounded by tall, straight, hickory trees on both sides and the back. It made sense that it would also mirror those trees, and rise up alongside them. A ranch house just would not do that. We wanted a second floor.

Olivia suggested an A-frame design, something like the Swiss Chalet houses she had grown up around in the mountains of Colorado. That made sense to me, also.

That would also let the house have a smaller footprint on the land, with a smaller, less expensive foundation, and a smaller, less expensive roof to cover the living area. Locating the bedroom on the second floor would also conserve heat in the winter, because the warm air would rise to heat it automatically. And we would not be paying to cover an attic that would not contribute to the living space.

The house would be open to the sun on the south side, where we would be able to take in the long views when the leaves left the trees in the fall. We wanted a lot of windows on that side, which would also let in the sun's heat in the winter.

But we also wanted to take advantage of the sun and views on the second floor, too. The solution was simple: Orient the gable end of the house to the south. That would open both floors to the sun and best views.

But orienting the gable end to the south would expose the house to a lot of sun in the summer. We did not want that. So, the design needed to incorporate a large gable overhang on the south side. A proper overhang would keep the summer sun, high in the sky, from entering without blocking the low winter sun from shining right in.

Because the house would be tall, the overhang would not be sufficient to shade the ground floor in the summer. So, we added a small deck on the south side that we could use as a sun deck, just outside of the bedroom. It would shade the ground floor in the summer, allowing the sun to stream in below it in the winter.

The Swiss Chalet design combined all of these features in a neat package. It was easy to see how it had evolved in mountainous environment, with many of the same features on our site. And it was a design that was familiar to Olivia, so she was comfortable with it. It did not take long for me to feel the same way. We would be building a Swiss Chalet.

What would the shape of the house be? I've always been a fan of symmetry, and of course the house would exhibit symmetry East to West. But if we made it a square, it would also be symmetrical South to North. The square floor plan would result in a simple foundation, and be pleasing to the eye. If we made the south gable overhang larger at the ridge than at the eaves, the house would be leaping forward to the sun and the south, and would do the best job of blocking the summer sun from the upstairs. A classic Swiss Chalet.

What would we build the house out of? Once I laid my eyes on those tall, straight, hickory trees all over the top of the hill, we immediately knew. We would be building a log cabin. Jack had quickly built a simple log storage building on Hannah's land, so I knew I could do it. And I had Hannah's house in Vermont to show me the way.

But her cabin, like most, was built from pine. Hickory is the densest and hardest wood in the forests of Southern New England, and it is notoriously difficult to work with. But I knew that cabins built from hickory had survived for longer than 100 years in the Southern United States. That was good enough for me. And someday far off in the future, long after the house had reached the end of its useful life, it would rot back into the earth, enriching it, instead of becoming a toxic waste site.

How big would the house be? We were not looking to build a status symbol. All we needed was a place to live. We knew that having more than we needed would not make us happy, quite the opposite. Without a lot of stuff to clutter up our space, we needed less space. Less is more.

We would be building our house of logs. Hickory logs. Heavy. It would be a good idea to limit their length. If many of them could be 12 feet long, that would limit their weight. A 24-foot square seemed to be the right size. Each side could be three 8 footers, or two 12 footers. It would yield 576 square feet on the ground floor. We could live in that. And we would still have the second floor under the roof, another 24 feet by 8 feet at least, for an additional 192 square feet.

The 24 feet by 24 feet square could be subdivided into 9 modules, each 8 feet by 8 feet, for 64 square feet each. The maximum span would only be 8 feet. Very symmetrical, very clean. The south wall divides into thirds, with a door in the center part, and large windows in the side parts.

The first floor would be open except for a bathroom in the northeast corner. An open floor plan is ideal to heat with a woodstove, and it would feel bigger than if it were cut up into rooms. The large room downstairs would function as a kitchen in the east-center module, and a large living room across the south facade. Just imagine basking in the sun in front of those windows on a sunny February day.

The upstairs would be a single large bedroom, with large windows on the south, and a door opening onto the small sun deck. Since the sun deck would be protected from the wind by the large roof overhang, I knew it would be comfortable even on a sunny March afternoon.

Producing the drawings catapulted us head first into the project. Now the project was taking shape in our heads and on paper. It was detailed. We had to begin thinking about a lot of things. My energy soared. It was time to get a building permit.

That's when the anxiety, and then the adrenaline, began to flow. How would our plans be received? These were not drawings that were professionally produced. And, of course, it was a little unconventional. I submitted my drawings, and held my breath.

It didn't take long. The meeting with the building inspector was short. His verdict: He liked our plans, but .... Our house was too small. Since we had submitted our plans, the minimum size house had been increased from 600 square feet of livable space up to 900 square feet.

I was shocked! A minimum size for a house? Wow, what possible damage could a small house do? Not absorb enough water because of the smaller footprint? Not consume enough fossil fuel to heat it? Not consume enough material in its construction? Of course, it was none of that. It was simple. A bald attempt to limit people of limited means from building in my town. Pure and simple, that's what it was. Make sure that no one who could creatively design and build a small house would be allowed to do that. I was stunned. I had been naïve.

What to do? Design a bigger house. We needed some place to live. We did not have the gumption to fight town hall on this one. It was the right decision for us at that time.

The easiest modification that we could come up with was simply to add another 128 square feet, two more modules. It would be an 8-foot by 16-foot sunroom off of the east side of the house. The room would have windows in all three external walls, and skylights in the roof. We would use it like an attached greenhouse. It would add humidity to the house.

I resubmitted our plans, and they were accepted this time. The building inspector did have some suggestions. He did not like my stone piers for the foundation, and required them to be poured concrete. And he wanted to see how I would seal between the logs. That was a good question. After talking with a brilliant manager at my local building supply store, I settled on his suggestion of using foam sill seal. After collecting the fee, the building inspector signed off.

We were on our way! Or so we thought.

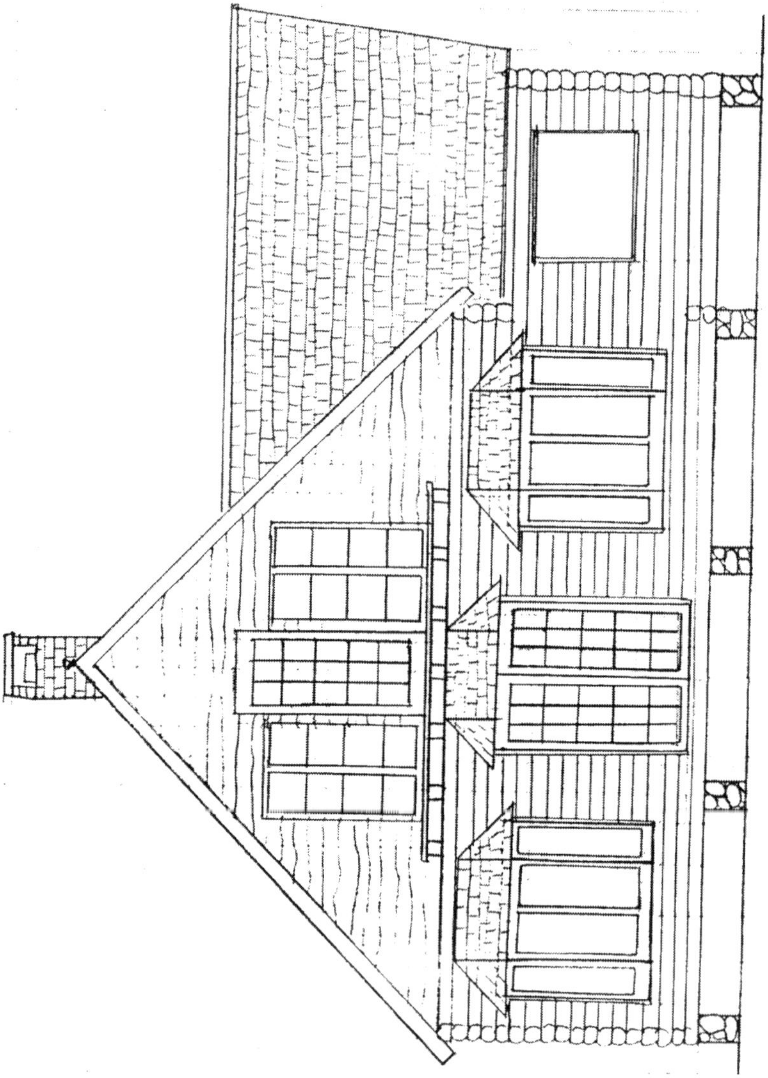

South Elevation

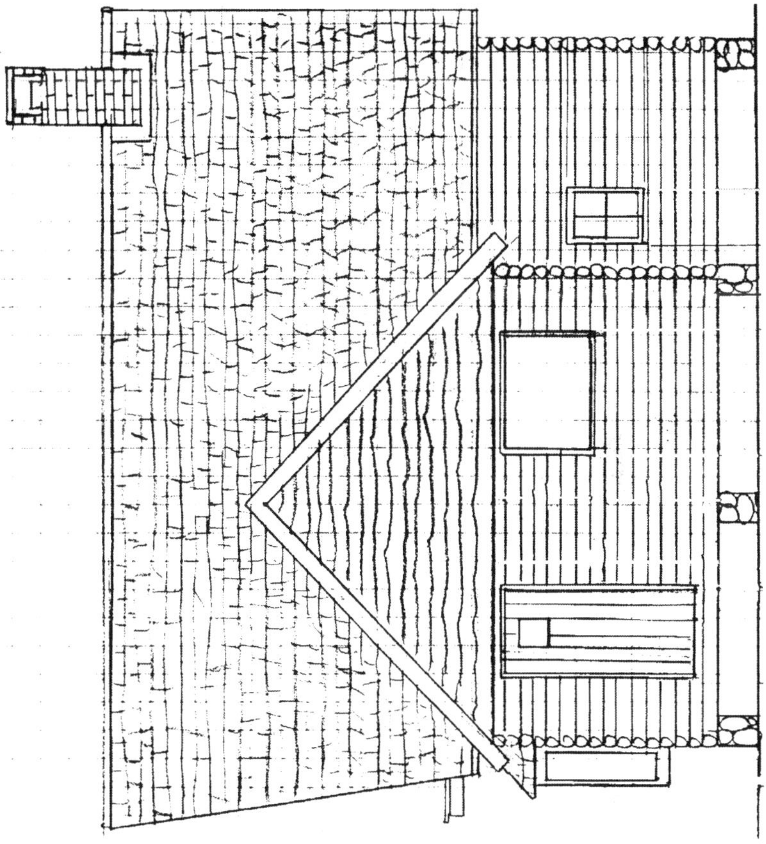

East Elevation

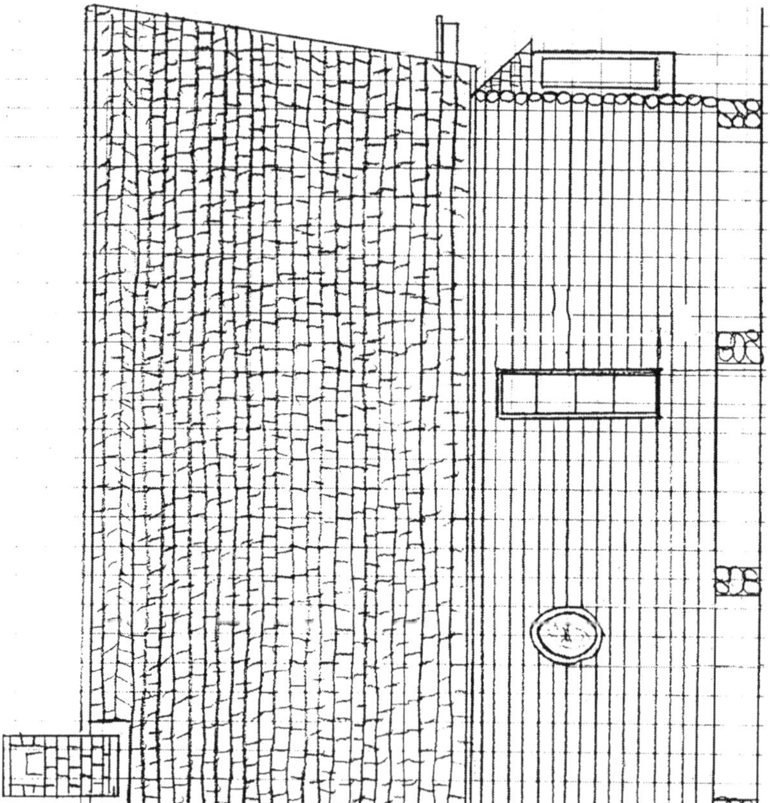

West Elevation

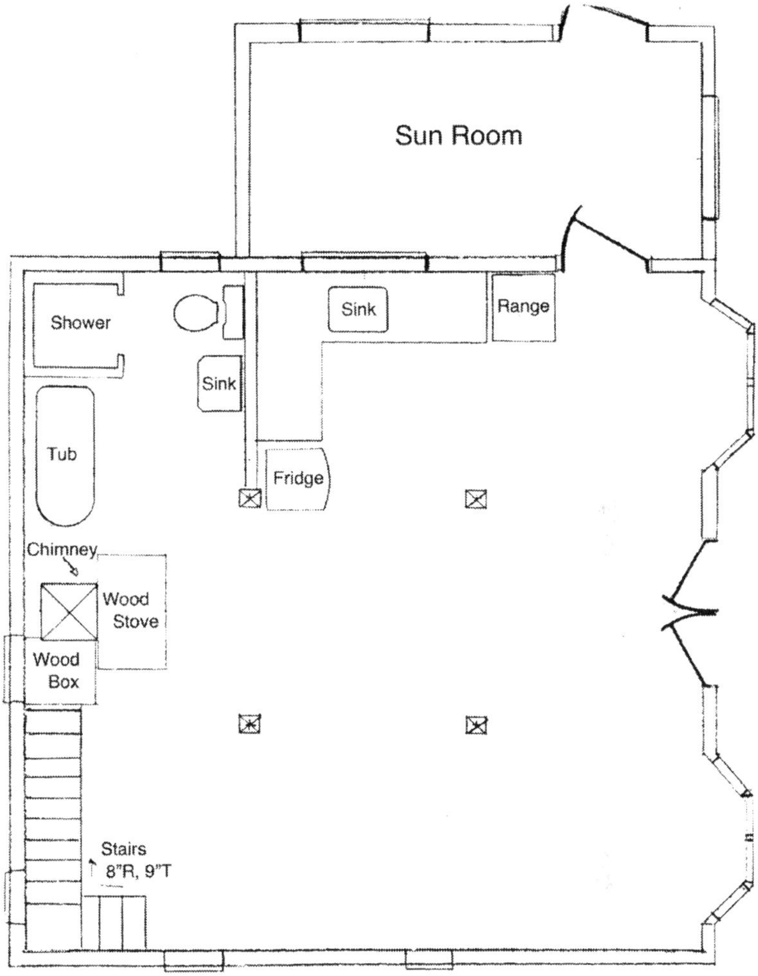
Sun Room
Shower
Sink
Range
Sink
Tub
Fridge
Chimney
Wood
Stove
Wood
Box
Stairs
8"R, 9"T

Floor Plan

A Fork in the Road

Finally, it was time. We had our land; we had our plans. It was time to locate the position and orientation of our home to be. Time to put some stakes in the ground. Yes, we were excited, but somehow the mood was strangely apprehensive.

Our backpacks were loaded with a hammer, ax, compass, hundred-foot tape, and a spool of cotton string. I used the ax to sharpen the ends of some side boards we had. They would mark the corners of the house.

Our home would be in the center of what was a long-abandoned field that had grown back to forest. There was a stone wall near the site that was oriented very close to North-South and East-West. That was perfect, since we wanted the house to be oriented to the south for maximum solar gain in the winter.

We drove our first two stakes into the ground, 24 feet apart, to mark the front wall. It was parallel to the east-west stone wall that would be behind the house. Then we drove two more stakes to mark the back corners. We measured across the diagonals, moving the back stakes until they all were 24 feet apart, and the diagonals were equal. That's how we knew the house was square. Next, we positioned and drove three more stakes to mark the corners of the sunroom. Then we stretched the strings across the stakes, marking where the outside walls would be.

We stepped back to look at the whole thing. It was the outline of our future home. I was excited, but Olivia seemed pensive, agitated. It did not make any sense to me. This was our dream. What was going on?

The next day, I found out. Rather abruptly, she announced, "I don't want to live up there with you on that hill." My shocked reaction: "Whoa, What? Why?" Again, her reply: "I just don't want to live there with you." We had lived together by then for close to 10 years. I knew her. She said what she meant. She would not change her mind.

But why? I really wanted to know why. Did sex have something to do with it? Yes, sex can get complicated. Olivia was sleeping with Jake when we hired him to log the land. Jack and I differ in one important way. He is straight. He connects with women in a way I never could. I knew that. Maybe that is why I was fine about Olivia and Jake.

When I met Olivia, she and Hannah were girlfriends, intimate girlfriends. I did not find that shocking, that she was attracted to women. I knew I was attracted to men. I always had been. But I knew I was attracted to Olivia, too. Was it the Frye boots? Her height? Her assertiveness? All of that. But to be crude, it was also tits and ass. And at certain times of the month, her pheromones drove me crazy. Made me very horny. For her. For her body.

But it wasn't just Olivia. I knew I was attracted to other women, too. But mostly, men. No doubt about that.

So, what did that make me? Was I bisexual? Gay? Straight? What should I call myself? You know, I didn't really care.

I hate labels. I endured hostility, one time physical, when I was visiting my boyfriend who lived upstairs of a gay bar. Someone on a motorcycle swung a heavy chain at me. And I endured verbal hostility in a gay bar when some patrons learned that I lived with a woman. They thought I was faking it.

I know that I am attracted to both men and women. I think many, maybe most, people do have some attraction to others of the same sex. Probably most just don't want to admit what they are feeling. For me, once I was honest with myself and others, my life opened up. I started seeing the world more clearly. I was far less constrained than I had been. I was in the company of Leonardo da Vinci and Michelangelo, both of whom had relationships with men.

So much for sex. But what about love? That was a big part of what Olivia and I shared. That is why Olivia encouraged me to explore my attraction to men. To share her lover with others. It was her love for me, because she knew it was best for me. That I had to do it. I loved her for that. And that she could not live with me up there on that hill with me. Not then.

As I write this now, 50 years later, I'm surprised how quickly I recovered from the shock. Almost overnight, my life had changed. I was not building that cabin for Olivia and I. Not anymore. Overnight. I knew it was me, not us. And that was fine. It had always been my dream. By the end of the week, I had moved out. And into the bus.

Beginning

It was time. I was going to begin the actual construction, and to completely submerge into my dream, for real. It was time to move onto the land. And into the bus.

The bus had been converted into a camper by a good friend Joe. When he moved to Key West, he needed someplace to park it. And we did have a spare 80 acres, so it seemed natural. I would park it on the land, and then live in it. It would be my home from now on.

Moving is always unsettling. Old routines will be broken. New places will need to be learned. I was moving into the woods. I knew and loved the woods, but I had never lived there before. I had a lot to learn. And for sure, my daily routine would be completely changed, too.

And I was living alone. It had been years since I lived alone. I had always enjoyed solitude, but living with Olivia, I learned that I definitely preferred living with someone. Sharing my life. And this was such an important time in my life. No question, I know I would have preferred to share it with someone. But that's not the way it was. I was alone, in the middle of the woods. In the following years, loneliness dogged me, some times quite painfully. But I was so busy, so focused on the project. It was my dream. That helped a lot.

Moving always has a physical exertion component: packing,

transporting, unpacking. Lots of work. But for me. it wasn't so bad. The only furniture I owned was a bureau with my clothes, and a homemade workbench. It was easy enough to remove the drawers, and move everything into the truck. When I got to the land, I simply backed the truck up to the bus door and reversed the process. I was moved in in about two hours.

With that done, I took some time to look around the campsite. Spring was springing all around, and I was too. It was early May, and the buds had expanded on the trees, and very few leaves were out, mostly on the low brush. But those new leaves were luxurious. The light green they were coated with had a satiny finish that glistened like ice at the right angle. They were perfect, as yet unblemished by insect holes or brown fungal spores. Tufts of grass in the clearing were greening up nicely.

Jack had driven the bus to the top of the hill, pointing southwest. He backed it into the woods, with a beautifully shaped dogwood tree by the front right tire. Everything was nicely nestled into the woods, just outside the clearing of the construction site. I would have a very short commute.

Jack had used the boom truck to hang the moving van pick up cap from four trees near the bus. He had built it to accommodate the belongings of a woman acquaintance he had volunteered to move. It had walls of thin 3-inch boards and a roof made of rubber waterproofing material. It even had a portion that was designed to protrude over the cab, like a real moving van. There it hung, waiting to be converted into my outdoor kitchen. That would be the project for the morning.

I was living in the woods now, and what immediately came to mind was camping. I did a lot of that hiking the Appalachian Trail. And the first thing I always did when I got into a shelter was to get water. Can't live without water.

There was a seasonal spring on our land in the bottom of the ravine. It was a pleasant 20-minute walk there from the bus. The path led across the high point of the ridge to the next hill top. There were nice views of the forested rolling hills to the south, since the land dropped off steeply from there. There was almost no sign of human habitation. Truly, I was living in the middle of the woods

From the hill top, the trail dived steeply down into the ravine. The spring was on the southern boundary of our land, at its lowest point. The water emerged from under a rock that was part of a rubble field the glacier had left behind, in the sag between the two hills. A friend had cleared the spring out, so there was a little pool of water. I had a drink of the cold, not too silty water. It tasted good. Then I filled all three of my gallon jugs.

In those days, I was used to simply drinking untreated water on the Appalachian Trail, so that's what I did at home too. That was before the days of widespread giardia. And then there was all of the deer poop down there in the ravine. So, it turned out to be unwise, and I changed my ways later. But back then it seemed to work for me, at least for a while.

Back at the bus, I filled my washbasin and washed my face and hands. Then I sat down on the bus bottom step with the door open, and ate a sandwich I brought. The birds had just begun returning from points south, so I was not alone as I sat on that step, absorbing the sounds and clean air of my new, hilltop home.

It was starting to get dark, so I moved in. I sat in the driver's seat, and enjoyed the last rays of the setting sun just outside the perfectly aligned picture window windshield. Then I lit a candle and just watched the flickering shadows ply across the bus ceiling and the emerging forest outside. It was incredibly calming, just breathing in the air, and feeling time flow. This was my life, and I was filled with tranquil joy. I had been dreaming about this for a long time, and now here I was. I slept well.

I woke up early the next morning, as the first red light of the new day flamed in through all those windows that surrounded me. At first, I didn't know where I was, but then I remembered. I was in the bus, my new home. And I was on my land. I was HOME! It swept through me in a wave of joy. I was HOME! I felt more at home in those fleeting seconds then I'd felt anywhere else before. Somehow, all the time I would spend here was reaching backward, embracing me, welcoming me, with a sense of recognition I did not understand. It was all strangely, immediately familiar.

And so, I began my first full day in my new home. I made a cup of coffee on my camping stove, and fried up some eggs. So far so good.

The project of the day was to finish building my kitchen. I would need to build a counter along one wall, with shelves below it. I had some hickory sideboards and 2" X 4"s from the mill, and I could easily cut them to length with my chainsaw. That part went easily enough. All that was left to do was to nail them all together. I thought I would be done before lunch.

It was not to be. The first nail bent after it went in 1/4 inch, and I could not get it out. The second, third, fourth, fifth did not go any better. I tried different nails. Same result. I was literally in tears. How was I ever going to build a house with this stuff when I could not even drive a nail through a 1-inch hickory board?

Eventually, I understood that I would need to drill a pilot hole first. That's how I finally assembled my rustic counter. It became abundantly clear to me that building the house was going to take a lot longer than I expected.

And it surely did.

The Bus

It was rust, but long before, it had been yellow. And in its day, it had been a "Superior Coach", as it proudly announced on a tarnished chrome embossed plate, to the left of the door. I doubt the kids riding it to school ever felt that.

The front door had been modified so you could pull it open by sticking your finger between the deteriorated gasket in the middle. There was a hasp for a lock, but I never used that. Once you passed through the portal, you were presented with the two steps to climb aboard, looking at the driver's seat straight ahead.

The back third or so of the bus was filled with the owner's stuff, blocked off with a sheet of plywood. I was just a nonpaying tenant, at that point. The bed platform stretched across the bus directly in front of the plywood sheet. There was a foam rubber mattress on top, covered with a sheet. But I never used real sheets on top of that. I simply used my down sleeping bag, sometimes as just a blanket.

My living room was in front of the sleeping platform, on the right side. It consisted of two rows of 2 reclining bus seats facing each other, from a 1950s era greyhound bus. A bench in front of the living room was a warm seat in the winter, directly across from the brooder wood stove that had once heated a chicken coop.

My workbench was behind the stove. It consisted of an old

door, over some large drawers filled with my junk. And my clothes were in an old dark blue bureau, between the bench and the bad.

It was a compact, but functional design. I could almost stand up straight, but not quite. But I could stretch out completely in the bed.

There was a row of 9 windows on each side that opened halfway by sliding down. I had plenty of light and air. I duct-taped screens to the outside of the bus, so I could almost keep mosquitoes out, but they liked to get in through the leaky door. When I first moved in, a branch from a nearby birch tree managed to sneak its way in through a window. I liked it, so I just taped the screen around it as it flourished above my bureau for a while.

My lighting system evolved considerably over my time in the bus. In the beginning it was candles, but that did not last too long. Sure, candle light is romantic, but it's just not very bright. Next step up was kerosene lamps. I had two of them, and that was better. Except, have you ever cleaned the carbon off a lamp chimney?

As I discovered, electric light is really the best. Clean, bright, instant. The bus already had 12 V lights along the ceiling. I hacked the bus battery into the bus control panel for the lights, and I rigged up a connection for my 12 V high-intensity lamp for reading.

I had a 40-amp Sears battery charger hooked up to the battery and plugged it into the generator. Whenever I ran the generator to work on the house, the battery was charging for free.

Another popular use for electricity was to run the radio. The bus came equipped with an excellent built in AM/FM radio. It was hooked to an antenna mounted outside the bus, so it was very sensitive. There were nights when I could receive AM radio from Canada and Mexico. And my hilltop location allowed me to get good reception of WGBH FM, the NPR station from Boston. For the first time in my life, I had access to a broader range of music than the local stations carried. I became addicted to jazz, and listened to "Eric In the Evening" almost every night.

I had electricity. What more could I ask for? Why not get greedy? How about a phone? Cell phones had not really been invented yet, so the only option was a land line. But it was almost a half mile to the nearest telephone pole, which was outside Hannah's. So, I ordered a phone line at Hannah's, and went to RadioShack to buy some wire. It would be easy, I thought. And actually, it was, in the beginning.

The phone company connection was through a box outside her shop. From there, I ran my 4-conductor indoor wire through the trees, relying on the branches to tension it just a bit. I ran the wire to a birch tree near the house site, and installed a phone jack on the tree. I placed a heavy stump at the base of the tree for my telephone table. Then I ran another wire over to the bus. I had a desk dial phone that I could move from the bus to the worksite, plugging it into the tree. Unlike on the old television show “Green Acres”, I did not need to climb the tree to place a call.

Everything worked fine, more or less, until the first stormy day. The wind would knock branches down across the wire, severing it. Then, after I spliced the repaired line back together, water would get into the splices. It was a pretty noisy connection, with a lot of squeals and pops. Later, after I had my little Macintosh computer, I was able to use the modem to telecommute a bit from the bus, but it was dicey. Better than nothing, though.

Because I eat so much, I really needed a kitchen. My kitchen was located alongside the bus. The cooking area was beneath Jack's moving van cap for his pickup, that we suspended from 4 trees. The whole thing was completely water proofed by a sheet of rubber that Jack tacked down on top. It even had an area that was designed to go over the cab. I used that for storage. I set up pallets toward the back to support my gas range and refrigerator.

It did seem rather preposterous to have a full-sized gas range and refrigerator in the middle of the woods, but at the time it seemed to make sense. I knew I would eventually need a propane range in the house, so when I saw one for sale on the side of the road, cheap, I made a spur of the moment purchase. I was able to run it on a 9-pound propane cylinder for several weeks. I did not usually use the oven, but I did like to make meatloaf and baked potatoes once in a while.

The refrigerator was more complicated. I knew I would not be on the grid, so I was looking for an old Servell gas refrigerator, which I could use during construction and later in the house. I would need to limit my electricity usage, so I jumped at the chance to acquire my neighbor Hank's ancient unit. Only five loads of firewood! What a deal.

It would have been expensive if it worked, but it did not. The Servell was a miracle machine: a solid, reliable refrigerator made in America that ran on propane. But it used ammonia, not freon. Ammonia is very corrosive, and it was an old machine. The tubing was leaky, and no one in my part of the world knew how to recharge it, much less fix it. So, I reverted to a Coleman ice chest. I froze gallon jugs of water in Hannah's freezer, and then drank the water that thawed out.

My dining area was just in front of the cooking area. I constructed a rustic dinette set from a heavy piece of slate that had been the top of a bench in a chemistry lab. It was set on 4 stocky tree trunks. On either side, I made benches from a plank I nailed across two more hunks of a tree. I could accommodate 4 for a sit-down dinner under the stars.

Generally, I got my water at Hannah's. I had a two-and-a-half-gallon jug with a spigot that I set on the end of the bench along the right side of the kitchen. When it was time to cleanup, I filled my large washbasin from the jug. Wash and rinse water were flung into the woods, nourishing the trees.

So, I had a bedroom, living room, work room, and kitchen. But where was the bathroom? That was easy. It was a shovel, with a roll of toilet paper over the handle, leaning against the side of the bus. The poop field was below the bus in a luxuriant stand of ferns. Every hole was at least 6 inches deep.

Maybe you noticed the shovel with the broken handle

leaning against the bus in the photo. Oh yes, I did break a lot of shovels. I bought the first one at Sears. It was a Craftsman brand, and in those days, the whole line was covered by a lifetime warranty. I've never been clear on what a lifetime warranty is. Is it warrantied until its life is over? What does that mean.

But for Sears in those days, it meant that if it broke, you got a new one. When I brought the broken one back to the store, the salesman looked at the shovel, then looked at me, and said, "Yes, I know. You've been blowing rocks. But that's ok." Then he handed me a new shovel, just like magic. I can't remember how many I got out of that initial purchase.

One thing the bus lacked that I really yearned for was a shower. In the earliest days, I marched into the woods down to a cold stream that ran year-round. It had some pools that were big enough to submerge into. The water was spring fed, gurgling out from under the hill in five places that converged into the stream. The water was very cold. Sometimes, on the hottest days, I would take my lunch down there and then dip into the stream to cool off. Fed and refreshed, I could go back to work. But thankfully, Hannah got her shower going before the weather turned cold, so I took advantage of that.

Another thing the bus lacked was an address. It can be a little disconcerting, not having an address. The land had an address, but not the bus. I got my mail through a post office box. Whenever I purchased anything at RadioShack, they insisted I give them my address. Not wanting to give away my PO Box, I simply told them "the bus". It didn't matter, their mail still found me. It's a small town.

The author between the bus and the outdoor kitchen

Oliver

It was the same every morning. An ear piercing, chest thumping, siren wailing of a chatter emanating 6 feet from my left ear, from the roof of my kitchen. Oliver was asserting his ownership of my kitchen and the top of the hill. Oliver the squirrel.

Just to make sure I knew who owned the bus, he would then jump down onto the bus roof with a metallic "plink", then it was the pitter patter of little paws as he raced down the length of the roof. If I was quick enough, I could catch a glimpse of him through the windshield as he slid down it to the hood, and then onto the wood pile near the front tire.

Within 10 milliseconds, he would emerge from under the dash, using a secret tunnel only he knew about, then jumping on the window ledge and racing along it down the length of the bus, passing inches above my head, before tunneling his way through Joe's stuff in the back of the bus, and then exiting somehow out the back. Every morning.

Oliver wasn't a particularly early riser. None of this "up at the crack of dawn" stuff. Not for Oliver. That was for the birds.

You will never experience dawn on a New England hilltop in April the way I did because that world is gone forever. The world will never again have the luxuriant density of birds that I had the good fortune to experience. A friend of mine from New York City said the morning chorus sounded like wailing fire engines.

It almost always woke me up, and probably Oliver too. I stayed in my sleeping bag cocoon and listened to the concert along with him, high in his hickory tree, as the first red rays of sun streamed into the forest canopy. Only after the climactic crescendo died down did he come down off his throne to harass me. He didn't want any competition.

I'll never know for sure, but I now think that I experienced Oliver even before I moved into the bus. Soon after we bought the land, I started clearing brush and trees for our driveway and house site. When I finished for the day, I left behind my gas can. It had a little plastic cap on the vent. The first night I left it out, someone ate the plastic cap. Now, I don't want to mention any names, but... Of course, it could have been the mice, who might have developed quite a taste for gas infused plastic.

As it got colder, I liked to enjoy a cup of hot chocolate from time to time. I kept the cardboard container of hot chocolate mix on the shelf at the back of the outdoor kitchen. It didn't take Oliver long to acquire quite a taste for it. His favorite brand was Swiss Miss. I wouldn't have minded if he had just been civil about it. But no, he went wild. He was wild. He would finish the entire can at a sitting.

I would show him. I bought a new one and put the unopened can in Hannah's big Coleman cooler. Wow was that a mistake! He just ate a hole right through the cooler big enough for him to get inside. He probably could've chewed through the metal skin of the bus if he had to. But he didn't have to. He already had multiple tunnels inside.

I never had to do hand to paw combat with Oliver, thank God. I'm sure he could have killed me. We had a truce of some kind. We shared his domain and he prospered. In flush years, when the hickories and oaks were loaded with nuts, his progeny became a plague. But what do you expect? They were there first.

Logs

Why logs? Because they were there. The first time I set eyes upon those trees at the top of the hill, I knew. This is how I could build my home, without a mortgage. I would use trees instead of lumber.

They were tall and straight, with no taper and few branches. Many were the right diameter, around 12 inches. It was easy to visualize stacking them on top of each other and chinking in between them.

But I knew that would be impractical for the winter. It would not be long before the wind would be whistling through. I really needed a flat surface on top and bottom to better seal them. Jack suggested it would be good to have the inside wall be flat too. That way if they proved to not provide enough insulation, I could fortify that with another wall inside. And when I planed down the inside surface of one of those hickory logs, the purple heart wood really looked like tropical hardwood. Maybe that's the way it would be.

There is just one problem: they were hickory. I had never seen hickory logs used in a log cabin. I knew that hickory was notoriously hard to work with. It is the heaviest wood we have, dense and strong. But it has a mind of its own, so watch out when it decides to bend or twist. I had read that there were hickory log cabins in Appalachia, some more than 100 years old. So, if you kept them dry, they could last a long time. That was important, because I did not want to use wood preservative, and breathe it in for the rest of my life. But still, I had my doubts.

The building inspector suggested I talk to an old man with Native American roots, who really knew wood. I talked with him, and felt better. He said for sure I could use them, but I would need to spike them together every two and a half feet.

Should I age them to perfection before using them, or use them green? What about the bark? Remove? When? Turns out all these questions were moot. I simply did not have the time or energy to age them or to take the bark off anyway. The only thing I knew for sure was that I needed to cut the trees down, strip off the branches, and buck them into lengths. Then somehow, I needed to get them to the mill where they would be cut flat on three sides. So that is what I set out to do.

I tried to select trees that were clustered together fairly tightly. That made them grow tall, with few branches. Fortunately, there were stands like that to the south of the house site. This was perfect, because I needed cleared space there to catch the sun for energy and the gardens.

Before you can cut down a tree, you better be ready. Jack's advice was to always park your truck where you could get out to get to the hospital, if need be. Of course, this won't help much if you are under the tree.

And you need to have a plan. Which direction do you want the tree to fall? Will it fit there? Can it get hung up in another tree? But even more basic, does it even want to go there? Hickories are very tall, and have a lot of leverage. The slightest puff of air on their tops can be enough to convince them to ignore your plans. I once dropped a hickory tree on my house.

Part of your plan needs to be your escape route. Since you are standing at the base of the tree that is starting to fall, you have to be sure you can get away. Fast. Don't get tangled up in a grapevine, don't trip on that root, and don't get caught under the falling tree.

It almost happened once. I was cutting cabin logs on the south of my house site. It was quite a steep slope, but the trees knew which way was up. Unfortunately, I did not.

The slope complicated figuring out gravity, and how it would act on the tree. I miss-judged the direction the tree would fall by maybe fifteen degrees, but that was nearly fatal. As the tree headed the way the tree was heading, I casually noticed that it was sliding into the big crotch of a tree maybe 15 feet away. That crotch acted like the fulcrum of a lever. The top of the tree went down, and the bottom of the tree went up. I calmly followed my escape path, never dreaming what I would see when I turned around.

The butt of the tree was flying through the air like a battering ram, aiming for my head. I jumped to the right, falling on top of the still running saw. In that instant, I had a quick visit from my grandmother, who had been dead for 20 years.

After the dust settled, I looked to the left. The butt of the tree was about 10 inches from my left ear. I turned off the saw. It happened so fast there was no adrenaline rush, no pounding heart, no spike of blood pressure, only grandma. I don't think I've ever been more grateful to be alive.

Usually, the tree will end up on the ground, but not always. Sometimes it gets hung up in another tree. Tremendous forces can be primed to snap back at you if you try to cut it. If possible, I would try to pull it down with my Allis Chalmers tractor, without tipping the tractor over. Other times, I had to cut through from the bottom so that the saw would not get bound up in the kerf as the tree sagged. And sometimes, I just asked Jack to bail me out. He could always get me out of the toughest tree binds.

Once the tree was safely on the ground, I would clip off all the small branches toward the bottom. At some point, there would be a large branch or crotch that seems like a good dividing point. I wanted the logs I harvested to have little taper from one end to the other. I would then measure the length from that discontinuity to the bottom, and try to divide it into logs of at least 8, 10, 12, or 16 feet. Actually, I wanted each to be slightly longer, so that I could put a notch on at least one end. I would want an 8-foot log to be closer to 9 feet and a 10-footer to be closer to 11 feet, and so on. Sixteen footers would be nice to build with, but they would be incredibly heavy, and I could never carry them in my pickup truck, with its eight-foot bed.

Once the logs were bucked into length, I hooked a chain on one end and dragged them to the house site. Often, I could loop the chain around each of two logs on either side of the cut. Then, when Alice pulled on the chain, the logs would (hopefully) fold around parallel to each other so I could pull both at once.

After I got them to the house site, I could use the boom truck I borrowed from Jack to load them. It was a Diamond T, built in the 1930s, and had been used to set telephone poles. There was a boom that could extend out several feet in back of the truck. The powerful winch could easily lift my logs 12 feet off the ground, once I got the truck started. It lacked an ignition key, or even a switch. You had to touch two wires together as they sparked, but she usually would roar to life.

So much for the cabin logs, which I would use to build the walls. I would also need lumber for the first and second floors, and posts to support the second floor. Jack said it would be possible to cut this lumber from the top logs left after my partners had him log their part of the land. Often, top logs are considered too small to cut into lumber, but Jack said they would be okay if I didn't mind a little wane with some bark on the edges. They were usually red oak, and would make excellent 2" X 8" floor joists, and various beams, and were already lying in the woods. It would be low-cost, high-quality lumber, once it was cut.

I worked with Jack to pull this together. Mostly I just walked behind the tractor, hooking and unhooking the chain. Jack said it saved him a lot of pain at the end of the day, by not having to jump up and down from the tractor.

Logging is hard, hot, noisy, dirty work, but it does have its rewards. The peachy, tart, aromatic aromas emanating from the fresh cut oak mixed with the moist leaf mold from the forest floor. The quiet, once the chainsaw was shutdown. And of course, just being in the woods was always a pleasure.

The logging went on intermittently for weeks. We accumulated quite a pile of logs waiting to be cut at a backyard sawmill. The mill sat unused while the owner searched for a part to fix the old Cadillac engine that powered his creation. So, we waited, and waited. Finally, it was time to start building, but still, no Cadillac.

That's when I hooked up with Gary and Henry, unincorporated. Jack met Henry while drinking at a local bar. Their mill was functioning, and they were willing to do the work. We would have to move all of those logs to the new mill. But we would not have the boom truck to load the logs.

Jack had a plan. We parked my 3/4 ton pickup parallel to the pile. Then we formed a ramp from two planks leaning against the side of the truck. Next, we hooked a cable to the underside of the truck, midway between the ramps. The cable ran under the log of interest, around it, and back up over the bed of my truck to the other side. Jack hooked his truck to the end of the cable, and drove away, perpendicular to my truck. Sure enough, like magic, the log rolled up the ramp and dropped into the bed of my truck with a bang. Repeat with each log, until the truck is full.

Unloading at the new mill was even more fun. Pull the truck up parallel to where you want the new pile of logs to be. Then, simply step on the gas, hard. If you are fast enough, you will partially spill the load, or at least de-stabilize it. Successive jabs at the gas eventually dumps the load, more or less on target.

So that was it. The logs were at the new mill, waiting to be cut.

Gary and Henry Unincorporated

"Gary and Henry Unincorporated", that's what was painted in bold white brushstrokes on the gray walls of the shack. It was humble, but for me, a lifesaver. I needed to convert those long straight, hickory logs into cabin logs. They would need to be cut flat on the top, bottom, and inside so they could be stacked like real Lincoln Logs. This was not something I would be able to get done at Home Depot, even if it had existed back then.

The mill they created was cobbled together by Gary, an ace welder, from ancient parts that had led a previous life deep in the forests of Canada, where he was from. It looked a bit casual, but once I got to know it, I realized it was a master monster piece of mechanical engineering.

The business end, or rather middle, consisted of a big four-foot diameter open blade mounted on one end of a heavy 2-inch diameter shaft. The other end of the shaft was coupled to a massive diesel engine from a caterpillar bulldozer, hiding in the middle of the shed. There was a double steel track that ran from one end of the mill to the other, just behind the massive blade. A long cart was mounted on the tracks that ran back and forth by the blade. It was driven by a cable that pulled it one way or the other, controlled by a big lever that changed its speed and direction. The cart could also be moved in and out to position where the log would be cut.

The input and output ends of the mill had no walls, just a shed roof. The logs were stacked on skids lying on the ground on the input side. Gary and Henry worked together to roll a log up onto the cart.

Henry would use a special yard stick to measure the logs diameter. The stick was calibrated in board feet of lumber. A board foot is a piece of lumber that is one foot square, and one inch thick. An 8-foot-long board, one foot wide therefore contains 8 board feet. Henry's stick estimated the number of board feet of lumber that would be produced from the log.

He was the uncertified accountant, and recorded the number of board feet of the log onto a pad nailed to a post by his station. The deal we had was that I would be paying 10 cents per board foot for the work they were doing. That was a very low rate. They decided it was fair because I was not having the logs cut into many boards. All we had to do is cut it flat on three sides, which was much less work.

After recording the board feet, Henry would sight down along the log, to try to get it as parallel to the track as possible. Then he would clamp the log down to the cart. Then it was Gary's turn, since he was positioned closest to the whirling, murderously scarry blade. While still sighting down the log, he would move the cart in, toward the blade, trying to position it so that the cut face of the log would have at least 6 inches of cut surface.

Then it was show time. Gary worked the big lever to slowly ease the end of the log into the blade. And it did sing like a cymbal as the blade bit into the log, and a jet of sawdust squirted down someplace beneath the workings of the mill.

Meanwhile, I was stationed on the opposite end of the mill, the output side. I did not have much to do so far. My prime concern was trying to avoid getting cut in half, since that blade really was not so very far away. I simply watched the log approach, trying not to let it push me over. When the cart had finally passed most of the log through the blade, I steeled myself for the impending drop, when the slab of wood was severed from the log. It would drop onto a long wooden table that ran along outside of the blade, from the blade to the end of the track, on my end of the mill. My job was then to pick up the "slab", and throw it onto the pile.

Each of those pieces that were cut off the side of the log were still rounded on one side, with the tree's bark still on, and flat on one side. The so-called slab wood had limited use. Of course, you could use it ornamentally to make a pretend log cabin by nailing it onto another wall, but that was not my thing. I was interested in the real log that was still sitting on the cart. But you could burn the slabs for heat, once it was dried out. I did save some to do that with. And Gary was able to use most of it that way, burning it in the big wood stove he had on the lower floor of his home.

Next step was to return the cart back to the input end. Gary and Henry would then unclamp it, and rotate the log 90 degrees so that the cut part was resting on the bottom of the cart. They then repeated their sight alignment exercise, trying to see if they could get at least 6 inches of wood on the cut surface again, moving the cart out.

Sometimes, if the log was particularly thick, Gary would attempt to predict the future. If he thought that he could cut a one-inch board off the log, and still have enough log left for a good cabin log, he would make a "side board". He indexed the carriage in one inch, and ran the log back through. The result was a 1-inch board with one nicely cut edge, and one edge rounded and with bark still on it, called wane. The board would flop to the table, where I would leave it. Sometimes, he was even able to get two side boards cut off the log. I planned to use those side boards to build my rustic furniture, which was easier said than done.

The final step in making the cabin log was for Gary and Henry to flip it 90 degrees again, set it up on the carriage, and clamp it down again. But this time, they not only had a nice flat bottom for it to rest on, it had a flat back as well. It was much easier to judge that final cut, to make a cabin log that was a nominal 7 inches thick from inside to outside.

After that final slab, and maybe a sideboard or two was cut from the log, it was my turn. I unclamped the log, now flat on three surfaces, and slid it onto a rough table along the track. I then slid it onto the bed of my truck, which was parked at the end of the table. There was a lot of friction to overcome, especially with those heavy 12 footers. Henry said that it looked like I was throwing them around like cabbages, but I struggled.

Once the cabin log was finished, Gary stacked up any side boards that had been produced, and ran them through the mill one more time to cut off the wany end. They were freebies to me, and I was grateful for their effort to produce them.

Sometimes even the big diesel struggled with my hickory logs. Hickory is notoriously cantankerous to saw. It is the hardest, densest wood we grow here in New England. Occasionally, the tree is stressed while it is growing, locking in a twist or curl of some kind. Then, when that log enters the big blade, all hell can break loose as it forces its desires on the mill. One time, a log managed to stall the powerful diesel completely. That engine had enough power to move houses, but my little 7" log taught it who was boss.

There really wasn't any place to store cut logs on the output side, so we only cut what would fit on my truck in one load. Henry tallied the board feet, and I paid in cash when we were done.

So, after working for a couple of hours on a Saturday or Sunday, they earned around $60 total, and I wound up with a truck load of cabin logs, maybe 25 or so. For me, it was my house, but for them it was mostly a hobby. The 10 cents per board foot was pretty cheap, considering that most native lumber back then cost 30 cents per board foot to cut. But we all enjoyed it, working together. And I think they really wanted to help me build my house.

But it was complicated. It always went much slower than I would have liked. It started with my phone call to Gary, "Can we cut wood this weekend?" Usually not, but once in a while, yes. Joy, another load.

After we finally got there, the first thing we had to do was awaken the mill and get it moving. The first step was up to me. I headed down to the stream to get some water for the big diesel. If it was going to freeze, they drained the water out after every use. That way there was no need of anti-freeze. Gary always asked me to be sure to filter out the pollywogs. He didn't want his radiator plugged. Then one of them would touch up the saw with a file.

Next there was the sawdust. Mounds of it. It tended to collect around and under the blade. If it wasn't too thick, we cleared it away with the snow shovel. But sometimes it was just too much to do that, packed solid around the blade.

Henry said no problem. He would get his backhoe and clear it away. We marched across the road to his farm. The backhoe was parked in the mud and manure, accumulating rust. It looked like it hadn't been started since the 1950s.

Before we could even try to start it, he needed to find a clamp for the battery. Again, it was "no problem". We walked into his barn, which sat at a 15° tilt, and picked our way through the stacks of stuff, to a tilted bench in a dark corner. It was coated in a 4-inch layer of nuts, bolts, nails, washers, widgets, and apparently at least one battery clamp, all dressed in oils of varying viscosities.

Then, when he tried to start it, not much happened. No problem, he said. I'll just hook the tractor to it, and pull start it.

I watched from the sideline, confidence ebbed. They hooked up the tractor to the backhoe with a chain and started pulling, with the bucket dragging along behind, making a new furrow in Henry's pasture. This went on for quite some time until they almost disappeared over the hill. Just when I had almost lost faith, there was a belch of black, sooty, smoke, and it started!

Henry drove across the road to the mill, and proceeded to the sawdust pile. Then he tried to activate the bucket, but not much happened. There was a hydraulic leak, so it just stayed on the ground. "No problem," he said. Then he swung the bucket along the ground, catching some sawdust on the side, and quickly rotated the machine, flinging the sawdust to the side with the injured limb. The process was repeated until the blade was clear enough to use. And then, after a three-hour delay, we started to cut logs.

Sawdust. I love the fragrance of it. We all did. I think it's one reason they ran the mill. Lots of sawdust at the mill came from cutting pine, and it smelled like Christmas trees. But my logs were hickory and oak. I like the smell of oak best. I could not really distinguish the smell of red oak from white oak, but both of them seemed to emit a fresh, pungent, pleasant aroma with hints of citrus and peach. The hickory was different. It had more of a biting, decayed smell. I once had a firewood customer complain because the load of hickory firewood I sold him stank up his garage. I used to call the worst of it "dog shit hickory". I guess you know what that smelled like.

Sawdust also has another use around a sawmill. It makes some of the highest quality mud imaginable when you lubricate it with some good, old fashioned New England clay. There was a wide moat of it around the mill, easily defeating 4-wheel drive trucks, when conditions were favorable for it. There were many days when we did not cut wood because we could not get to the mill.

Once the logs were cut, I needed to get them home. They ranged in length from 8 feet to 12 feet, but my truck's bed was only 8 feet long. "No problem," as Henry would say. You just put the 12 footers on the bottom, and then stack the eight footers on top. That should hold them, and it usually did. But one time...

I had been carrying sand the day before, and there still were a few ball bearings of it between the truck bed and the Homosote sheet protecting the bed. Naturally, the whole load of logs was stacked on top of that conveyor belt. Fortunately, it was not far to my house, and it was all on back roads. Unfortunately, there is one steepish hill. And I had been rather aggressive in my load, taking a lot of 12 footers.

I started up the hill in second gear. Big mistake. About halfway up, I knew I had to downshift, so I did. That's when the load slid back. Very soon, my front wheels lifted off the ground. Now I could not steer. Could not go back. Could only go forward. So I did.

And then, snap, pop, and the whole load sat there blocking the uphill lane, still stacked perfectly on top of the Homosote sheet. Then the front wheels of the truck hit the ground, so I could steer again. I just stared at the pile of logs blocking the road. Rather embarrassing. I knew that I needed help.

I raced up the hill to our land. Hannah was hosting her annual Memorial Day roundup, so I knew there would be a lot of women there, some stronger than me. A quick call for volunteers, and I had 4 strong women in the bed of my truck. We headed down the hill, and stopped near the pile.

A chunky, shirtless man holding an open can of beer was in front of his Cadillac, just below the pile. "Is this your wood?" he inquired. I sheepishly admitted to being the owner. He just laughed, and backed down the hill so I could position my truck below the pile. Then he watched in amazement as we moved the whole pile onto the truck in about 30 seconds, and I backed up the hill to deliver my load.

Just another day cutting logs, but one I will remember forever.

Banks

Finally, we were ready to go get our mortgage. Or so I thought. We had our land. I had my logs. I had my bricks. We had done our homework. We had building plans that were approved by the building inspector. We had a building permit.

And I had excellent credit. Part of my homework had involved how best to prepare for getting a mortgage. So, even though I did not need it, I borrowed $600 in a useless loan for money I did not need, and paid it back on time, just to develop good credit. And then I borrowed money to buy a car, which I paid back on time. I had done all of my banking at my local branch of the Connecticut Bank and Trust, so that they would get to know me. I had done my banking homework. I was ready.

I walked into the bank, full of confidence. After a short wait, I was escorted to a loan officer. It was a man I had never met, but he sure looked like a banker. I pulled out our drawings, and held my breath.

I didn't have to hold it too long. After glancing at them for about 3.5 seconds, he laughed. "Oh, I'm sorry sir, we could never loan you money for THAT!", he announced. There was a lot of emphasis on the last word. It was my dream. I was crushed. I gathered up my documents, and my ego, and marched right out the door. I was angry. 'THAT' was my dream, after all. I did not even want to drive by that damn place again. But I did need money. What to do?

After a couple of weeks, my ego began to heal somewhat. I was still angry, but some of the anger was directed at me. I should have known better. But still, I did need the bucks. I screwed up my courage, and marched back in there again. This time, I asked for a loan to buy major appliances. After all, they had already loaned me money before. I asked for $10,000. It was a different loan officer this time. He simply asked if I already had the funds to build the house. I answered in the affirmative. I got the loan. Of course, the major appliance was the house itself.

And so, I built the house with the loan money. It was not too difficult making the payments, far less than what they would have been for a mortgage. And I was free to build it anyway I wanted. No bank would ever tell me what to do again. And I didn't have to devote 30 years of my life chained to that bank. It was good for me.

For the Connecticut Bank and Trust Company, not so much. It became part of the Bank of New England, which generated a $1.2 billion loss in 1990. The loss was attributed to poor investments in the real estate market. In 1991, the FDIC seized the bank and placed it into chapter 7 bankruptcy liquidation. The bailout cost the FDIC, meaning you and me, $2.3 billion.

Too bad they thought I was such a poor risk.

Fort NASDAQ

It was my first day. I was the new consultant, still trying to figure out where the bathroom was. And it was quite different from living in the woods. You swiped your badge to enter in front of the guard from Bridgeport who wrote poetry. There were no windows to the outside, except for one in the cafeteria. But there was a glass wall looking into the massive machine room. It was filled with rows and rows of computer racks loaded with 80s era minicomputers and assorted peripherals. On the other side was the office, filled with cubicles. Old-time engineers were walking around with packs of cigarettes rolled up into the sleeves of their T-shirts, and usually with a pencil behind the ear.

I was in the building where NASDAQ (National Association of Securities Dealers Automated Quotations) was invented and first built. It was the world's first electronic stock market. They collected and instantaneously electronically published data from numerous stock exchanges. Their customers were brokers around the world.

It seems they needed my help, and I certainly needed some of their money. So, four days a week, I drove an hour and a half to get there. I put in four 10-hour days, Monday through Thursday, and slept in a motel for three nights. On Thursday, I returned to the bus.

My first day was in August, hot and muggy outside, but how would I have known? I was hermetically sealed in air-conditioning. Until I wasn't. Suddenly, in midafternoon, the lights flickered and alarms started going off. Lightning had knocked out the power. People were more than a little concerned, but they told me not to worry, there was a back-up power supply. A jet engine next to the building would start up to keep the whole building going. And in the meantime, a whole room full of batteries would keep the computers running.

But it did not go well. The jet would start up, then within a minute shutdown. Over and over. But the machines kept running. That was very important. A lot of brokers were paying a lot of money for uninterrupted service.

The machines did keep running, but unfortunately, the air conditioning did not. It was not on the battery backup, and it was getting hot in there. Next thing I knew, men were on the roof of the building, wetting it down with firehoses. A decision had been made to keep the machines running until 4 PM, when the New York Stock Exchange closed. Any toasted machines would be rebuilt overnight. And just at 4, the power came back on.

My new colleagues wagged their fingers at me. "What did you do, Sievel? What did you touch?" I knew it could not have been my fault. I had not touched anything. Yet. So, I thought they were pulling my chain. But I wasn't sure. I would do my best.

There were only two of us working on the "old" network. Thomas was the other, also a consultant. He lived on Long Island, so for him the commute was arduous, involving a ferry ride. He had negotiated the four-day work week as a way to minimize the commute. In fact, if he had not already pioneered the four-day week, I doubt they would have let me do it.

We had been hired to keep fixing the old network while almost everyone else was working on the new network. Seems there was this upstart by the name of Bloomberg that was trying to steal the business. The new network was a response to that. While Thomas and I toiled away patching up the old system, the other engineers got to design the future. That was fine with us.

There was no room for us inside Fort NASDAQ itself, so we were assigned to some trailers behind the building. Thomas and I shared a large cubicle, back-to-back. We had decent chairs, but most of the rest was improvised. We created a lot of furniture made out of computer printouts in our cube. Stacks and stacks of it, 132 columns wide. We each had a dumb terminal on our desks hooked to a Digital Equipment Corporation VAX machine, and some pencils and pads.

Thomas grew up in England, and still carried a lot of it in him. He was always attired in a suit and tie. It's what he was most comfortable in. And meanwhile, I was in jeans and boots. But we instantly hit it off.

There was a badge reader guarding the back door to the main building, and we were constantly going back and forth through it. Often it would not recognize our badges. But Thomas had a way to tickle it to make it open. It was like this well-dressed businessman could so easily break into the British Museum.

There were a couple of rituals on the days we shared. We took turns running out to the local health food store for broccoli bundles for lunch. Then we would take our lunches across the road to a nature preserve. We hiked on a forest road to a bucolic pond where we ate lunch. For me, it was incredibly important to get out of the hermetically sealed environment, into the woods again. And it established a daily walk and became Thomas's typical routine. Years later, he told me that he was the only person in Los Angeles that walked to work.

The other ritual was our 3 PM sugar fix. We took turns running out to the bakeshop. For me, it was usually hot chocolate and a danish pastry. Thomas liked coffee.

What exactly were we doing? We were modifying existing code to fix problems, or add new features. If you are not interested in the gory details, you might want to skip ahead a bit.

We were assembly language programmers of Data General minicomputers. Mini computers were smaller than the big mainframes. Microcomputers were not yet very available. Data General was a company that was started by engineers from Digital Equipment Corporation, the first mini computer company whose computers were widely used. Data General computers were cheaper.

The boxes we used were Data General Novas. They fit in a rack, and were about 1 foot thick. They had 64KB of memory. Just to give you a sense of scale, that's one millionth of the memory of a 64GB phone. And one of those old computers could run maybe 64 brokerage terminals. We got a lot of work out of that memory.

Usually, there was no room to squeeze in any more new code, since the memory was already packed solid, every bit used. We had to rewrite some existing code to make it use less memory, so we could shoe horn our code into the space that was freed up. And then, of course, it was necessary to adequately test what was rewritten, to make sure we had not broken it. All of this before you could even start your task. But we had a lot of time, and we needed a lot of time.

We programmed in assembly language. That's very close to the bare metal of the machine. You have instructions like ADD 3,4, which tells the machine to add the contents of register number 3 to register number 4. You can do anything if you have enough memory, which of course we did not.

We edited files on the big VAX system using the terminals on our desks. When we were ready to test the code, we used a program on the VAX that was a cross-compiler. It produced binary code designed to run on the Novas, that was punched onto cards. Then you took your deck of cards to the test machine, which read them and pretended to be an actual Remote Data Center. It had live ticker lines from the actual exchanges, so it was a popular place to watch the markets. But of course, it was always running raw, new, untested code.

There was no operating system on the Novas. There was no room for that. There was just raw driver code that was assembled in. You could change that too, if you dared to. A lot of constraints, but a lot of freedom, too.

And the "networks" hooked to the machines? They were basically pairs of copper wires rented from the phone company. And the communication protocol? Complete homebrew. Internet protocol (IP) had not really been invented when all of this was built.

Most of the peripherals were custom made. One of the more interesting was a magnetic drum storage system. Instead of a platter, like a disk or CD has, it had a large drum in a big box, bigger than a washing machine. The drum was coated with a material that could be magnetized, like an old tape recorder. Except that instead of having just one read or write head, it had one for each track around it. It was like spinning a horizontal ear of corn very fast, and having a whole row of read/write heads, one for each track around the ear. It was much faster than a disc platter, because you did not have to wait for a mechanism to move the head to the correct track. Instead, you just switched to the head for the track you were interested in.

They kept those drums spinning all the time. Apparently, one time when they restarted one that had been stopped, the bearings seized, and the drum broke free, smashing through its enclosure, and a cement block wall, just for good measure. Sorry I missed that.

One of my tasks was to develop the WHP command (pronounced whoop, as in whoop it up). The technicians already had a WHO command, which would display information about who you were, such as the port, etc. But they wanted the same information for the PCU, programmable Control Unit. That was the device that actually drove the brokerage terminals. So, I tapped into the WHO call code, reusing its detection of "WH", and branching depending on the next character being "O" or "P". Memory was that tight. And, as usual, I had to find some sloppy code to rewrite, to fit everything in. It was a seething cauldron of octal code. It took weeks.

After I had been working for a full year, I was entitled to a two-week vacation. That was great: finally, some time to catch up on the house. But when I returned after the two weeks, I was shamed. Many index fingers crossed over, shame, shame. I had broken the whole system. It was an intermittent problem that was extremely hard to track down. Turns out I had turned all instances of "2" into "3".

How did I manage that? The nova computer had what is known as a zero page. It was the first 128 locations of memory in the machine, and had the distinction of anyone being able to get at it from any place in the machine. It was a handy place to store things that you might need in many places. Things like the number "2". So, I used the literal "2". Then later in the code, I needed a "3", so I simply incremented the "2" to a "3". Problem was that for all the other code on the machine, “2” had actually become “3”. Anyplace you think you had “2”, you now actually had “3”. That caused quite a few things to go haywire.

I will always be in awe of the old-time engineer that figured that out. A whole lot of intuition. Modern computer languages have guard rails to keep you from stomping all over the machine. But not back then.

So, I was deeply embedded in the abstract world of bits and bytes for 40 hours. When Thursday evening rolled around, it was enough, time to get out of there. I usually drove an hour or so before breaking for dinner at a highway truck stop. It was late, and tired, harried people were at the counter.

One night, a man with a cast on his leg limped over on crutches and sat next to me. He was building his own house, but fell off a ladder. He was under extreme pressure because of time limits on his mortgage. He was trying to finish the work, hobbled as he was. I had so much empathy, and a lot of gratitude. I could have been in his shoes if the bank had given me what I had asked for.

And so it went, back and forth to the fort and the bus. And that jet engine shut down on my first day? It was a squirrel stuck in the air intake. Maybe a relative of Oliver?

Foundation

Finally, it was time to start building. It was becoming clear that we actually did own the ground where I wanted to build. I had a sample load of cabin logs. It was time to break ground for the foundation.

Most houses in our neck of the woods have a full concrete basement, but I did not want to go in that direction. First off, it would be expensive. I did not have a mortgage, and would be building mostly out of pocket. At that time, I felt that a full basement was a luxury I could not afford.

Also, I did not want a basement because I thought it would be too disruptive of the water table. I would be relying on a shallow, dug well, and not a deep, drilled well. I did not want to disrupt that with a full basement. And, cost was important. A dug well would be a lot cheaper.

Instead, the house would be built on piers, 19 of them. They would be square, and needed to extend 42 inches below the ground. I would need to dig 42 holes, perfectly aligned, of course, on 8-foot centers. How tough could that be? I did consider hiring a back hoe to dig them, but decided against it. I did not want all the looseness and disruption around the piers that a backhoe would produce. And again, money. I would hand dig them. How tough could that be?

Much tougher than I expected, it turned out. The top of the hill is a drumlin, a big pile of glacial till sitting on top of the bedrock. I've been told that the till was deposited when the glacier melted directly over my house site, dropping its fullest load right there. So, bedrock is a long way down there. The till is a mixture of rocks of all sizes, embedded in clay, sand, and gravel. It is what is known as "unsorted" because you never know what you will run into at any depth. Unfortunately, I did not know any of this when I started digging.

The first 16 to 18 inches was relatively easy. The top 5 inches was black dirt, threaded with rocks and roots. Below that was sandy loam, a mixture of sand and clay, with embedded rocks. Then you hit the clay layer at 18 inches. Water only slowly percolates though it. It is hard, doing a fine job of gluing everything together. At that depth, a shovel is useless. You need a heavy bar to loosen it, and a post hole digger to lift the "dirt" out. Unfortunately, I did not know what a post hole digger was, so we scooped the loosened dirt out with an old pan, reaching deep into the hole. It was a very dirty job.

True, there is some dirt, but at least as big a volume of rocks. If you are lucky, you loosen around them and lift them out. But more often than not, they reach far beyond the edge of the hole, leading to Alice's Wonderland. What do you do? Expand the hole from above? That's a lot more digging. Sometimes you just tunnel into the side of the hole, trying to loosen around it.

How big are they? Every size imaginable. Unsorted, after all. We had to use Allis Chalmers to move one that was about the size of a kitchen table.

Surely there must be a better way, I thought. So I went to the rental place, and borrowed an auger with a gasoline engine. It had an 8-inch business end that would love to chop off your foot, and was easily capable of that. But one thing it was not capable of dealing with: rocks. Depending on size, they could quickly stop the auger from rotating. Of course, the rest of the machine, with 203 pounds of me attached, would continue to rotate around the hole, dragging me like a stinky, sweaty sock.

Sometimes I stood my ground, and the machine broke. I wound up returning 2 of them before they finally gave me one that was stronger. It went painfully slowly.

But help was on the way. Layla, and her new girlfriend from Holland, had expressed a desire to help me build my house. When we first started talking about it, we all had visions of notching logs together, building a log cabin. That's what was supposed to be happening by now. But that never took into account Ralph Bigbee's long lost son, and his hold over my land. So, we could not start the foundation until August, when the land issues were finally resolved. August, a great time to be digging holes in the hot sun. But they were game.

Usually, I rose at 5 am to try to get some work done in the cooler hours. But Layla and her partner were newly co-joined, bedded down in the camper at the edge of the woods, languishing in matrimonial bliss. They usually arrived around 10 as the temperature approached 90 degrees, and I was ready to quit for the day. But we got it done, somehow.

Originally, I had planned on building my piers of stone, but the building inspector was not too impressed with that idea. He insisted that I use poured concrete instead. Hannah offered the use of the forms she had used for the piers of her shop. They were 12" X 12" X 60", and made of pine. I loved them. They really made the job easier. I just modified them for each hole. I suspended them off the bottom of the hole. That way, the concrete would spread out of the bottom, filling the bottom of the hole, and forming a wider footing for them to sit on.

But there weren't enough, so I made more from some of the side boards I brought from the mill. Finally, I decided to use Sono Tubes: giant toilet paper tubes 10 inches in diameter, for the ones in the middle of the house. They would not need to support the heavy weight of the log walls. I custom cut them to length with the chainsaw.

I had to decide how far above the ground the top of the

foundation should be. I wanted 18 inches or so above the dirt, high enough to keep the wood off the wet dirt. I choose the highest ground, and made that my reference. My site was pretty level, so they were all about the same height above the ground.

I used a water level to get all of the tops of the forms at exactly the same height. A water level is nothing more than a small tank of water with a hose coming out of a hole in the bottom. I set the tank in the middle of the site, and filled it with water. I adjusted the height of the tank so the water level at the end of the hose was at the reference height. Then I simply walked around to each form, adjusting it so that its top was at the same level. I just cut the tops of the Sono Tubes off at the right level.

Once all the holes were dug and the forms were in place, it was time to invite the building inspector for the foundation check. He took all of five minutes, glancing into the holes, and measuring one or two before he signed off.

The only smidgen of sanity that snuck into my plan was that I would not try to mix my own concrete from cement, sand, and gravel. I would buy ready mixed concrete.

Pouring day is like final exam day. The 52-ton truck is sinking into the mud, ready or not. If it gets stuck, I will need to hire a bulldozer to get it out. I was warned about this during my building course years ago, and when I placed the order. Are all of the holes done? Are the forms strong enough? Are they braced enough? Are they aligned? At the correct level?

The concrete was already hardening in the truck, so I had to get it in the holes pretty fast. Then suddenly the truck was empty and I almost did all of the piers. For the one that was left behind, I could mix my own concrete later. I inserted the rebar that would letter secure the first logs, and smoothed off the tops. Then, I collapsed, exhausted, into my hammock as a light drizzle moistened the new piers. Perfect, slow drying conditions.

I slept well.

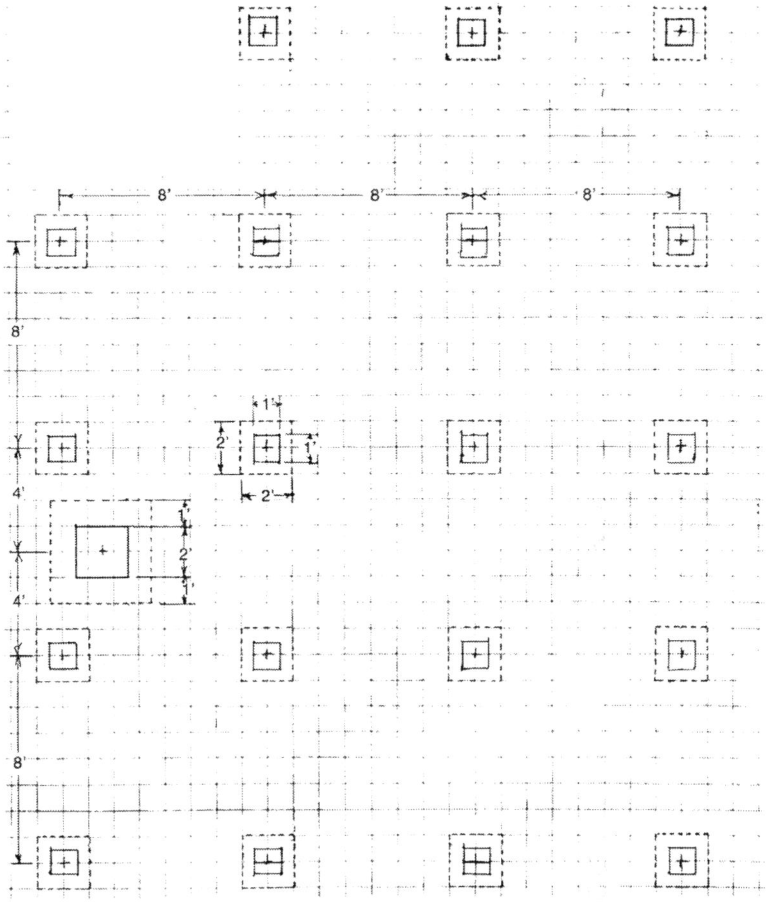

Foundation

First Wood

Foundation work is dirty. We spent maybe three weeks, working underground, with our sweat gluing the sandy loam, and worse, to our bodies, usually bent over on our knees. And what did we get for all of that? Just 19 small obelisks, 15 inches tall, in a grid pattern aligned fairly closely to the sun. But now things would be different. I would be building "on" the ground instead of "in" the ground.

It was quite impressive when you viewed it from the side, on a diagonal. Each obelisk had one or two little pieces of 3/8" rebar sticking out of the top. And at a little before 1 PM (daylight savings time), their shadows aligned almost perfectly. Solar energy would be a major part of this house, and it was already working.

First thing I needed to do was support the floor. It would be built from 2" X 8" oak floor joists on 16-inch centers. I would need some beams to support them. I decided to have some of the larger logs I got from Jack cut on top and bottom only, 8 inches thick. I left the raw tree on both sides, since it would be visible as the first log of the house on the outside.

It was a good plan. Too bad I hadn't thought of it earlier.

The sawmill was clogged up with cabin logs, waiting to be cut. These would be different, considerably thicker. So, we had to roll them over the pile of hickory logs waiting there. Brute force to the rescue.

Once I got the milled logs back, the work moved right along. The trickiest part was drilling the holes in the bottom of the logs for the rebar to fit into. I held the log in perfect alignment over the re-bars and gave it a whack with a 7-pound mall. This usually left some indentation where the rebar sunk into the log. I turned over the log, and that's where I drilled the hole.

Then it was time to start up the generator and drill the holes. I used a 3/8-inch ship auger bit. It was the first time I had ever used a ship auger bit, and I was really impressed by how well they worked. There is a small screw thread on the tip that bites strongly into the wood. Behind it is a kind of chisel scraper, and then a long auger to lift the chips out of the hole. They drill fast, and can drill very deep. Mine were capable of drilling down 17 inches.

I only had to drill 5 inches or so deep, just enough to accept the rebar. But as you might expect, the logs rarely slipped over the rebar. If I didn't hold the drill exactly plumb, or the rebar was not exactly plumb, or the logs were not exactly square, things might need some tweaking. But when you are working with stuff this big, tweaking might entail the drill, the chainsaw, and the heavy maul, used as a hammer.

So now that I had something for the floor joists to sit on top of, I needed to have a wall 8 inches high to enclose them. I relied on some larger oak logs, cut 8 inches thick, and flat on the top and bottom. The outside of these logs remained natural, since they would be visible on the outside of the house. But on the inside, I cut 2-inch notches with the chainsaw, every 16 inches, to accept the ends of the future floor joists.

I did not want to build the floor just then, and expose the plywood to the elements for who knows how long. But when that time came, I would be able to slip the joists into the notches, and nail the plywood floor on top of my new logs, up against the walls, which would rest on top of them. The floor and walls would be tightly tied together.

With this course, I did not need to worry about rebar anymore. I would simply position the log where I wanted it, and drill 3/8-inch holes through it into the course below, every few feet. Then I would use a larger spade bit to make the top of the hole an inch across, so that the head of the pole barn spike I was using would recess into the hole. That was necessary because wood shrinks. I was working with fairly green wood, so it would shrink quite a bit. If the heads of the spikes were not recessed, they would hold the top log up as the bottom log shrank in thickness. The house would be drafty as a wind tunnel, up there on top of the hill.

These first logs were a rehearsal for the walls to come. It was a chance to try to develop some skill with the chainsaw in making good square cuts. And the drilling, counter sinking, and hammering would soon become routine. I was enjoying the hard physicality of the work, as well as the careful attention to detail. I loved working with the fragrant oak.

I was finally building my house.

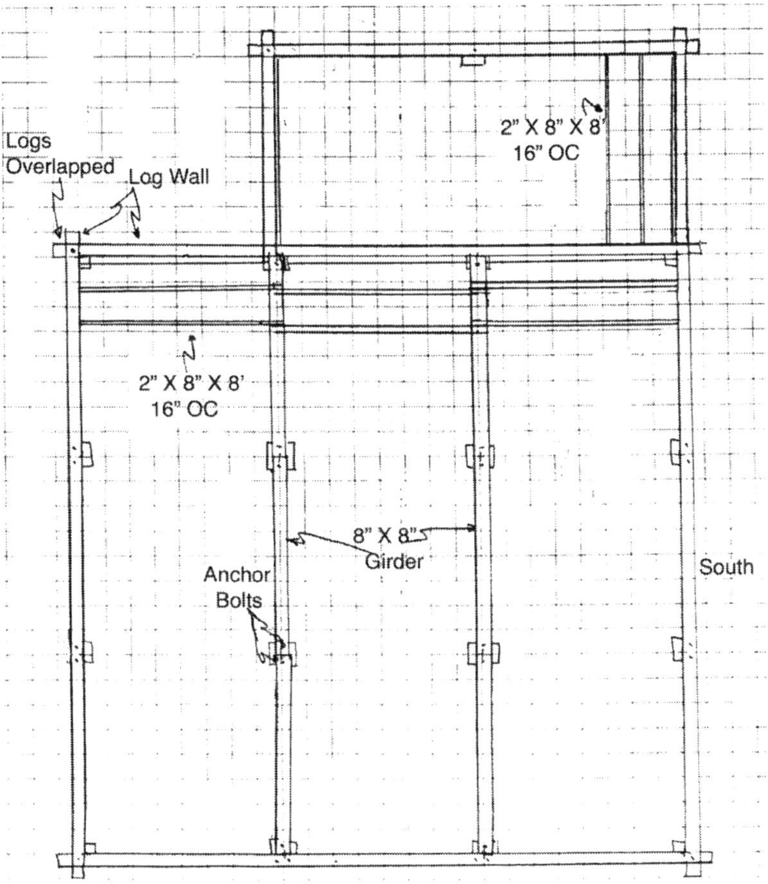

First Floor Framing

Log Walls

Building the log walls was the most significant part of the whole project. My house would not be a log cabin if it did not have log walls. It's not too surprising that building the log walls required more time than any other part of the project. It was primarily what I worked on in the fall of 1984 and the summer of 1985.

First, I had to decide what log went where. I had to look at the characteristics of each individual log to see where it would fit best. That was a lot easier when I had a good supply of logs.

Before I could build the log walls, I had to get the logs up on top of them. Usually, I liked to set a full course of logs on top of the existing walls, all around the house. This would supply enough for a couple of days work. While the walls were not too tall, I was usually able to lift them, one end at a time, onto the walls by myself, as needed. I would place them kitty corner, across two adjacent walls.

But as the walls grew taller, and also for logs 12 feet or longer, I needed help. A 12-foot hickory log weighs about 200 pounds. That help arrived with the "Happy Hooker", Jack's 1930's vintage Diamond T truck that he loaned me. Years ago, it had been used to set telephone poles. On the passenger door, painted in white, flowing letters, it said, "Happy Hooker". It did not have a key, or even a switch to start it. You just held two wires together, and if the arc did not burn your fingers, the truck would start. Almost always.

If I did not have any help, I would need to do the hookups and drive the "Happy Hooker" myself. That was tricky, I would drive the truck over to the pile, and play cable out of the winch. Then I would jump down out of the driver's seat over to the pile, pass the hook at the end of the cable under the middle of the log, and hook it back to the cable.

Then it was back in the truck, and lift it slowly. Of course, while it was ascending, that's not all it was doing. It liked to spin, and have one end tip down. It was especially tricky with the 12 footers, since they were long enough to swing right around to the boom on the truck.

And lift it all the way to the top. That was to shorten the cable, because the next step was to drive over rough ground. That log was prone to swing wildly, and the short cable minimized that. I would have to go very slowly, to not let any crazy motion of the log build up.

Approaching the wall was the most delicate part of the operation. The goal was to have one end of the log end up on the wall where it was supposed to go, and the opposite end resting on a perpendicular wall, a short distance away. The cable would be lowered so that the new log was just above the wall where it was to go. Then, I would reach out and stop any motion, and position it exactly, then lower the cable, and hold my breath. Usually, the log wound up on the wall, and did not slide off.

The whole operation got more and more complicated as the walls got higher. Towards the top, I had to reach up with a stick to stop the log from spinning, and to position it properly. It was especially difficult if I did not have any help, and had to hop back into the truck to lower the winch. It was a little like a kid's game, trying to use the controls to snag the toy. The timing was critical to actually have the log drop right onto the wall as it spun.

Setting the logs was usually a Friday thing, or it happened whenever a "guest" dropped by to say hello. I would put them right to work, either driving the truck or guiding the logs into place. I also got some help from a young boy, Eugene, that I hired for a couple of hours a week. He was far more skilled at controlling the truck than I was. And I think he was the artist that named and painted the "Hooker", but it could have been Jack.

Eugene was only 12 years old, but he was much more skilled than I was at controlling equipment. I remember Jack watching Eugene maneuvering the truck around smoothly. It was such a contrast with my own jerky motion. It seemed that all the horsepower of that truck just amplified my clumsiness. Eugene made it look easy.

Getting back to the logs, they were cut flat on the top, bottom, and inside. They were 6 inches from top to bottom, and nominally 7 inches thick from inside to outside. The basic idea is pretty simple: stack them on top of each other.

The tricky part is the corners, where walls are joined together. The corners add rigidity, so that a wall is much less likely to move in and out. To accomplish this, the logs from each wall are interwoven and pass through each other. Last time I looked, it was impossible for two logs to occupy the same space at the same time, so you might expect that part of each must be cut away.

This can be done if the logs on one wall are exactly a half course below those on the intersecting wall. Then the bottom half of one log can be cut away so it can pass over the top of a log from the opposite wall, which is a half course, or 3 inches, below. The logs from each wall take turns occupying the corner.

Notice that I said that it was the bottom half that would be cut away. This is important. If you cut away the top half, any water that got into the joint would flow right down into the notch, rotting the log. But with the notch on the bottom, any water that got in would just flow over the top of the log below, rather than into the notch.

The first step is to position the log that needs the notch directly over the intersecting log below. Generally, I put a 3-inch block under the opposite end, so that the log would be level. Next, I traced the outline of the notch onto the sides of the log.

The inside edge is easy, because the logs are flat on the inside. I used my level as a straight edge, transferring a line that is plumb from the corner below. As always, it needs to be 3 inches into the log.

The outside edges of the notch are trickier because the logs are not flat, and have a profile the notch will have to accommodate. I used a divider tool to do this. It is like a compass, with a point on one arm, and a pencil on the other. The arms were locked 3 inches apart. Then, each of the two outside profiles were traced onto the log to be notched by following the curve on the log below. The idea is to shift the profile up so it will be in the correct position on the log above.

Once the edges of the notch are drawn, it was time to cut it. First step was to flip the log over so I could work on it. This was a tricky operation with just one person. I had to be sure that the opposite end remained on the wall. The bigger logs were far too heavy for me to lift back up on the wall if they slipped off. But the end where the notch would go could be rolled onto the adjacent wall. So I went to the opposite end, and snap-rolled the log, trying to not dislocate my shoulder. Then I put the 3-inch block under the non-notched end, so the log would be level.

I used my chainsaw to cut the notches. The inside of the notch was easy to cut: just a straight cut down 3 inches. But the outside edges were more complicated. Because the logs were usually fatter in the middle then on the top, I approximated that by making a series of cuts from the outside edge, down to the traced profile line. Then I made a series of cuts across, maybe one quarter inch apart. I knocked these semi-disks out with a hammer, and then used the saw to "polish" the bottom of the notch flat.

Next, it was time to flip the log over and test the fit. This time, there was a satisfying clunk when the log dropped into place. Or not. Sometimes I needed to figure out what was wrong and repeat the whole process. More often, I could fine tune the notch with my chainsaw.

So much for the notched end, but what about the other end? Sometimes it was also notched, because that wall segment was only 8 feet. Then I would lay out and cut both notches together. But if the non-notched end needed to connect with another log not at a corner, I had more work to do.

I did not want to simply butt the two ends together. That would be a disaster, with the cold wind whistling through when they shrank. I decided to use a ship lap joint. I cut a notch on the inside surface of one of the logs from top to bottom, 3 inches deep, and an inch long from the end of the log. On the mating log, I cut away 3 inches of its outside, from top to bottom, one inch shorter, so the logs could mate. That way, there would never be a straight path through the wall.

Once all the notching was done, it was time to fasten the logs to the wall. But before this, I needed to install the gasket material. A knowledgeable manager at my local lumberyard recommended that I use sill seal, a plastic foam like material I could buy in large rolls. It is usually used to seal the junction between the concrete foundation and the first wood of a normal house. I stapled the sill seal to the top of the log below. I also used the sill seal in the notches, both at the corners, and the ship laps. It compressed nicely and sealed very tightly.

It was important to be sure the walls were vertical, so I constantly checked the inside edge for plumb with my level. If it was not right, I shifted the log in or out slightly. Once the position was correct, I clamped the log in place with a set of large clamps that cabinet makers use to make doors and countertops.

Anchoring the logs in place was the most satisfying and fun part of the whole operation. I used 3/8" X 10" pole barn spikes, positioned 2 1/2 feet apart. The holes were drilled with a long ship auger bit and my electric drill, which I ran on the generator. I also had to enlarge the top half inch or so of the hole large enough so that the head of the spike recessed into it. I used a spade bit with my drill to do this. If I did not do that, the spike heads would be sticking up when the logs shrank, preventing the log on top from sealing tightly.

The most fun part was driving the spikes with a 7-pound mall. A dab of dish soap on the spike tip eased the job. It was satisfying work, without the roar, smoke, and dust of the saw, drill, or generator. And I could hum John Henry as I worked on the railroad.

So much for solid log walls. But my house needed windows and doors, too. It would be passive solar, so the south wall would have three large windows and a double door. In fact, there were sections of the south wall between openings that were only 2 feet long. Without notches, they would be very wobbly. Something needed to be done.

The problem was solved by inserting splines into the ends of the logs around the openings. I cut the opening square with the chainsaw, and made sure it was plumb inside. Then, after three courses had been stacked, I positioned the chainsaw above the top log, and slowly cut a 2-inch-wide notch 2 inches deep, 2 inches from the inside edge of the opening. I made several cuts and removed the wood with a chisel.

This time, though, the notching was a lot tougher. I was cutting into the end grain of the log. I was ripping, not cross cutting. It's much harder to rip than to cross cut. Jack taught me to file the saw teeth perpendicular to the chain's travel, so the tiny teeth were acting more like chisels than saw teeth. Even so, there was so much friction that I could often see sparks in broad daylight. And plenty of smoke, even though I cranked up the oiler on my chainsaw.

After the walls were up, I would hammer a 2" oak or hickory spline into the end notch. I made sure to leave space at the top to accommodate the shrinkage of the whole stack of logs. The weight of the house above, along with the spikes, would keep the logs tight, and the spline would keep them plumb.

The splines also provided a place to anchor the door and window frames. I did not want to attach them to go logs, since I knew that they would keep moving as they shrank. But the splines were much more stable.

The walls took time. In a seven or eight-hour day, I could only expect to do a little more than halfway around the house with one course.

Though very physical, with a lot of heavy lifting, the repetitive work was somehow relaxing. It was so gratifying to see the walls of my house rising higher, day by day.

An Honest Day's Work

Work was done. The tools were put away. The generator off. It was quiet, and the late afternoon light sublime. The sharp, clear, fall air was filled with the fragrance of hickory and oak chips. The trees glowed their colors brilliantly, spotlighted by the low beams of sun.

As had become my custom at the end of the day, I enjoyed contemplating the day's work, often over a smoke. Usually, there was a close examination of the notches I had cut in the logs, checking their accuracy, seeing if I could have done better. But this day was different.

For the very first time, two walls were now high enough to begin sheltering me. I sat on a plank placed across two temporary floor joists that had been inserted into their notches in the lower logs. I was at the future level of the floor, and leaned my shirtless back against the rough log walls, sanding my back on the wall, like a bear rubbing up against a tree. It was good. I soaked up the warmth of the sun as the shoulder high walls protected me from the cold north gusts. I was home, sheltered at home.

The satisfaction of building home is primeval, deep in our

genes. We all need shelter, and have been building it for almost as long as we've existed. I was using natural materials obtained from right here, the way we have been doing for millenniums. And satisfying on a practical level, too. I would have someplace other than the bus to live.

Sitting there, looking at what I had created, felt a little like being in a hologram. It floated there in front of my eyes, the way it had been suspended in my mind's eye before. But this was real, tangible: I was sitting on it. It supported my weight and stimulated my back and sheltered my body. Real, knock-on-wood. For a software engineer that normally deals with abstractions, it was very satisfying.

It's real, and real heavy too. A 12-foot hickory log weighs around 200 pounds. I would wrap my arms around the middle, and trundle it over to the walls while my arms got longer, or so it felt. If I did not dislocate my shoulder, a quick snap of my forearm would flip the log over. Then, there was holding the heavy chainsaw within 1/16 of an inch as it grabbed the wood. Finally, every log was drilled every 2 1/2 feet, and a 10-inch spike pounded in. The heavy work more than satisfied any need I had for exercise. If you have all of your exercise needs met by your work, you are truly lucky.

I built it with my arms, my legs, my back. But mostly, I built it with my hands. My hands guided the tools, guided the logs. They were the enabler. From thought to being, from idea to reality.

I am often struck by how little respect many have for those who work with their hands. Maybe that's because so many people have no experience at all working with their hands. That is so, so sad, and a real hole in their education.

One publishing company I worked for once required all new management hires to take a one-week course, working in most departments. I was terrified when it was my turn, working in the press room, to tape a leader on a 1-ton roll of newsprint. At the right time the leader would be slapped against the running roll. If you did it right, the press kept running. But if you did it wrong, the whole plant shut down. It sure grew my respect for the press men that did this every night.

When I suggested the one-week exposure to another company I worked for later, they said it would be of no value. But they are extinct now.

A log cabin relies on its corners for strength and stability, but the junction will be weak and the house drafty if the corners are not tight. This requires great care in tracing and cutting the notches. A heavy chainsaw is fast, but difficult to control with precision.

I did get better as the walls went up. The top of the wall does have the tightest joints. As my skill level improved, the workmanship got better and better, and that was hugely rewarding. Anyone who has developed that kind of craftsmanship should be proud, and should be very respected by all, but especially by those who have never worked with their hands.

So, all of those thoughts and feelings flooded into me on that perfect afternoon. I had put in a good day's work, satisfied with what I had accomplished. I was honest with myself, too. I knew it was the best work I could produce.

I was building far more than a home. I was building a life.

Firewood

While I was busy building my walls, the earth was busy with what it does, too: moving around the sun. The season was changing. As September morphed into October, the bus was starting to get quite cold by morning. It had almost no insulation, and plenty of windows. I longed for a cozy fire.

Hank had a suggestion. He was a former neighbor and an ardent junk collector. Hank had a full yard of treasures that overflowed as he tried to lay in even more. He had an old wood stove that had once been used to heat a chicken coop. It was compact, and would be just right to heat my bus, he reasoned. And the cost? A load of firewood.

I'm a sucker for a deal. Are you kidding? Firewood? I had that coming out of my ears. There was wood left over from clearing the house site. There was wood left from clearing the road. There was wood left from clearing the future septic leach field. And there were the ends of logs that got cut off. There was slab wood.

So very soon, I had a cute little brooder stove hooked up, behind the driver's seat, with the stove pipe exiting through a panel in the window. And I started accumulating a woodpile by the right front tire, just outside the door. By this time, I had completed Jack's Firewood 101 course, so I understood how easy it was to split ash with my 7-pound mall, and I knew I could burn it green, too, if need be. It sure felt good to toast my buns by that fire.

But Hank was not done with me yet. He was a bit of a slum lord, and owned a four-apartment cement block hovel that he rented cheap to students. And it included heat: wood heat. He had a boiler on one end, and would stoke it up every night before he went to bed. Only thing he needed was, you guessed it, firewood.

Well, I was hooked. I went shopping in his outdoor showroom. He had a fiber glass tub-shower enclosure that I thought I would need. Cost? Three loads. Then I found out that he had an old Servel gas refrigerator that does not need electricity. Five loads. Etc. Load after load after load. No wonder it took me three years to build the house!

Meanwhile, it was getting colder. Hannah looked at me and said, "You're going to spend the whole winter in the bus, aren't you?"

It's not something I had intended to do. I had investigated renting an apartment in a nearby complex. But I did the math. The rent I would pay in two years was about what I would need to build the shell of the house. Now that I had heat, the bus was feeling more and more like home.

Firewood has been a part of my life since the days of the oil crisis, in 1972. That's what it was, a true crisis. The price of oil quadrupled in one year. You could only buy gasoline every other day, based on the last digit of your license plate. I had been renting a house in Hank's neighborhood. Previously heat had been included in the rent, but the landlord could no longer afford to do that.

It seemed absurd to me to rely on something that had to come from so far away for heat to survive when we were surrounded by wood. We bought a woodstove, and Hank let us cut firewood on his adjoining land. And it felt so good, too. I was hooked.

So having enough forest land to provide a renewable source of heat became part of the dream. Managed properly, the forest would thrive, and I could be forever warm.

But it did more than that. With the amount of forest we had acquired, there was more than enough to sell firewood. It was like money in the bank.

Well, not exactly. There was a lot of work involved, but Jack taught me. First step was to scan the classified ads. (Remember them?) in the local paper to see what the going price for seasoned, not green, firewood was. Then I would choose a price toward the bottom of the competition. I would be selling wood that was cut and split to the customer's specifications. The longer the pieces, and the larger around, the less work for me. If someone wanted wood cut very short, say 14 inches, or less then 5 inches around, I would need to charge more. I limited the delivery area to within 10 miles of my town, and specified cash only. I placed an ad and waited for the orders to pour in, which they always did.

Since I was selling seasoned wood ready for use, I needed to find standing dead trees, or trees that had been down for at least a year. My woods were usually filled with such wood. Mother Nature is a grim reaper. And then there were all the tops from Jack's logging, already on the ground and dry. I had more than I needed.

Tops were the easiest. Most of them were at least partially suspended in the air, so they were dry. And since they are the thinnest part of the tree, less splitting was involved. The trailer filled fairly quickly.

Standing dead were more work. I would try to drop the tree across some other chunks of wood to keep them off the ground. If my calculations and luck were good, it would suspend itself with the end extended out over a rock or a log. Then all I had to do was go down the length of the tree, cutting it according to the customer's specifications. If I was lucky, the cut off pieces would fall on their ends, just begging for me to split them.

If I was unlucky, the tree would suspend itself across two

supports, like a bridge. Then I had to carefully cut it in half, cutting from the bottom to avoid pinching the saw in the log as it started to sag.

If I was stupid or really unlucky, I would get the saw stuck. Then I could look forward to maybe hours of work trying to get it out. Usually that meant taking the saw apart, first repatriating the body, then maybe the bar, and hopefully eventually the chain. But I had other chains so I could reassemble the saw with another chain, and try again.

I did not have a wood splitter in those days, so I relied on my 7-pound maul and brute strength. There is a science to trying to figure out where to hit the piece. You look for small cracks, and you look for strait grain. If the piece has a large branch coming out of it, the grain of that would be oriented across the grain of the tree. It would be very difficult to split. If it was a large crotch, I didn't even try, but abandoned the piece in the woods, letting it rot to enrich the soil.

Momentum is everything in splitting wood. You really want to get the mall moving as fast as you can, without pulling apart your elbow or shoulder joints. I like the mauls with wood handles best because they dissipate some of the shock when it hits. You keep hacking at it until it splits, or your limbs give out.

Sometimes, you just can't make any progress. I had steel wedges for that. You get them started in a crack, and pound them in with your maul. Eventually the log splits, or the wedge is permanently embedded in the wood, only to be released when you burn it up.

I rarely used my wedges in the woods. If the piece was that hard to split, I could not make any money. I left them in the woods to rot and nourish the soil.

Once the trailer was filled, or more likely, overfilled, I climbed up onto Alice's (a 1949 Allis Chalmers model B) broad upholstered seat, and looked forward to a few minutes of "relaxation", wrestling with the steering wheel.

My logging road was very crude, so I had to guide Alice carefully as she wove her way through the trees, and bumped over fairly big rocks the glacier had decided to put just there, pulling on my arms savagely as I gripped the wheel with both hands, hanging on like my life depended on it, because it did. The logging road ended on the driveway, where I could pull alongside my waiting three-quarter ton pickup truck. It took around 1 1/2 loads to fill the truck.

Once the truck was full, it was time to deliver the load. That's when I got paid, usually, hopefully. I did enjoy cruising around in the truck with a load of wood in the back, listening to country radio. And meeting customers was "interesting".

My least favorite turned out to be the farthest away, apparently ignoring my 10-mile rule. Since I was already there I started to unload. I threw out one piece that had a broken end, like when the wind had broken off the branch. The customer looked at it and said, "I don't want that. It's rotted." "It's not," I replied, but I threw it back on the truck.

After I got about half of it unloaded, he said he did not want to pay the full price. Jack had warned me that this would happen at some point. Selling firewood involves a lot of work. I knew my price was low. I could not lower the price anymore.

"OK," I said, and started re-loading the truck, just as Jack had recommended. Suddenly, the customer said he was reluctant, but would take the wood after all. I unloaded the wood again.

When I was finished, he wrote me a check. Well, my ad clearly said cash only, but I just wanted to get out of there. Two days later he called to order three more loads. I told him I was sold out.

My favorite customer was a man that owned a big wood furnace in his basement. He wanted 4-foot lengths, with very little splitting. And he ordered five loads. When I brought the first one, he came out in a pouring rain to help me unload, and he told me how good the wood was. He made my day.

Wood season started mid-September, and ran until I could no longer do it, usually in November or December. As the season progressed, the fall rains turned the woods mushy. Alice was not 4-wheel drive, so it got more difficult as she skidded her way through the slimy woods. It was especially tricky getting back up out of the ravine with a full load on the trailer.

Sometimes, I could get a bit of a reprieve in December when the ground started to freeze at night. Often, it was solid enough to navigate in the morning, but turned to mush again by noon. The days got really short, so there was not much time to work. Into December, snow usually shut down my firewood empire.

I remember one late November day. I was struggling to fill my last order. The wood was down in the bottom of the ravine. The snow started just as I was starting to load the trailer. By the time I got it loaded, there was 3 inches on the ground. I plopped my butt down onto the snow-covered bench, and managed to coax Alice out of there. Exhausted, I got into the house and peeled off my wet clothes, through some wood in the stove, opened the damper, and collapsed in front of the stove. The heat surrounded me. Wow, what a relief! Soon, I was sound asleep, glad that wood season was over.

But by the next September, I was out there again, year after year, eager to get going again. It is my life.

Winter

It was getting colder, wetter, darker. The days grew very short. It was difficult getting anything done, either on the walls or cutting firewood. As I struggled with drilling a log on the wall, I heard an engine rumbling up the driveway, and looked over in that direction, as it started to snow. A Cadillac emerged out of the snow squall. When the car stopped, a well-dressed woman wearing high heels emerged. It was Agnes, the local tax assessor, carrying a clipboard.

She seemed to not notice or care about the blowing snow or the mud. But she sure was interested in the generator, which was howling away. "Oh," she said, "You have a generator," and she make a note on her clipboard. "And there's the bus," as she pointed to my new home, with smoke billowing from the pipe out the window. Another note. Then she duly recorded that the boom truck was there. Finally, she made a quick measurement of the wall of my house, not more than 3 feet high. And she told me not to worry, I would not be charged full price since it was still under construction. Another quick look around and she got into her caddy and drove away.

Like small towns everywhere, my town was always short on

cash. Most of it went for the school, with a little left over for the volunteer fire department, highway department, and transfer station. We are a frugal town, and one of the first in the state to institute recycling. The paper and cardboard we separated out paid for two teacher's salaries in those days. We all try to save.

Agnes was doing her job, and was good at it. She was in charge of valuing your real estate, motor vehicles, and personal property. The real estate values were derived from the size, kind, and finish of your house and the land. The motor vehicle value came from a blue book. She got the info for the registered vehicles from the state. But if she found a junk car parked out in the woods, or a school bus, watch out. You would pay for that, too. And she went after everything. She was not well-liked in town.

She was not particularly interested in the obvious fact that I was living in the bus illegally. After all, I did not have a certificate of occupancy for that, but she didn't care, so long as I was charged the twenty dollars or so a year for the bus. I would have been more relaxed if I had known that then.

And so, as winter closed in, so did I. It was time to abandon my outdoor kitchen. Usually, the wind was so strong it blew out the burners on my gas stove anyway. About the only use I had for my outdoor kitchen was the storage shelf at the back. As it got colder, I could stock frozen food right there on the shelf.

I cocooned by my little brooder stove, and it became the center of my life. It was a cast iron barrel, about 3 feet tall, and a foot and a half in diameter, with a square box at the bottom for ashes. The ash grate just above that was missing an arm that allowed it to be dumped, so I bent a replacement out of one of my 10-inch spikes. There was a little trap door on the top to load it.

The stove pipe also came out of the top, and then turned 90 degrees via an elbow to exit through the window that was filled with a cement board panel. Then the pipe turned another 90 degrees outside, topped with another 4 feet of stovepipe.

The pipe was stabilized by three wires at 120-degree spacing, attached to nearby trees. When the wind blew, as it often did up there, the whole assemblage creaked like a pirate ship at sail.

The stove was located behind the driver's seat, behind a small partition. I needed to protect the wood paneling of the walls from the stove's heat, and had the perfect material. I had a pile of my prized, 100-year-old bricks, with children's finger impressions in them, documenting the child labor that had been used to produce them. I built a brick wall in front of the paneling, and placed a sheet of metal on the floor. The bricks would also store some of the heat, averaging out the temperatures in the bus a bit.

My three days in the bus every week began when I arrived from Fort NASDAQ Thursday night. If the snow was not too deep, I could drive to the top of the hill. Usually, it was around midnight, and of course the bus was frozen solid. I would go into the bus, open the stove damper, and kindle a fire. I always kept some computer print-out paper and dry kindling wood under the dashboard in front of the driver's seat to make that easy.

Once the fire was going, I would grab some dry logs from under the dash board, load up the stove, and go back into the car. Then I would run the engine to heat it up, and turn on the heater full blast. After a half hour or so of listening to the radio, I could retire to the bus, which was toasty warm by then. I could get it as hot as a sauna, and often did.

By then, it was close to 1 AM, and I was exhausted after a full week's work, and the long drive. I submerged into my down sleeping bag toward the back of the bus, and slept soundly.

When I woke up in the morning, the bus would be an ice box. I slipped on some clothes, then opened the damper and stoked the stove, filling it to capacity. Since I was burning hickory and ash, there always was a load of coals in the bottom, so it usually caught quickly. I filled the kettle with water, and headed back to the sleeping bag.

In half an hour, the bus was toasty and my coffee water was

boiling. I made my instant coffee, and started on breakfast. Usually, it was three eggs, fried in butter, with a couple slices of toast. I made the toast in a skillet on top of the stove. Then I could look forward to a relaxed morning by the stove, reading or doing homework.

I kept the fire going through the day, bringing in more wood from the pile outside, by the right front tire. Lunch was usually a sandwich, or two or three, sometimes served with a side of a cup of instant soup.

Dinner was the big meal of the day, and I often ate it with Hannah at her place, or a local restaurant. But if I was dining at home, I usually opted for a "boil in bag" meal. That was so simple: no cleanup. But sometimes I splurged on a frozen dinner or family sized lasagna. I perfected a way of simulating an oven on top of the stove in a large pan on a cookie cooling rack.

You might think that refrigeration for my meager supplies was not much of a problem in the winter, but that was not necessarily true. Initially, I would store my milk, water, lunch meat, etc. on the bottom step of the bus entrance. The door was leaky enough so that it usually was about the right temperature. But as the season progressed, I found that I needed to go one step up. And finally in January, the floor of the bus was plenty cold enough. In fact, often too cold: milk frozen solid was sometimes the result.

I used to use contact lenses in those days. I would remove them at night, and place them in their case, filled with saline solution, near the stove. But one morning, they were frozen in the saline solution. From then on, I moved them into the sleeping bag with me at night, so my eyes would not freeze up in the morning.

It wasn't just the cold, though. I was on top of the hill, with nothing near that was taller. The wind roared across the hill at times. The bus squeaked and groaned like a Viking ship as the stove pipe circled around.

One night, while I slept, the stove pipe worked itself loose, and fell against the wood paneling. As the paneling smoldered,

I woke up to a smoky bus. I tried to get out of my mummy sleeping bag, but, as usual, the zipper was stuck. So, I bunny hopped down to the door, and out into the snow. At least I was still warm. I grabbed some snow and put out the fire. I shut down the stove, and hopped back into bed.

Most of the time, I was able to get up the hill in my front wheel drive Honda Civic. It was amazingly nimble, clawing its way through the ice and snow. But there were a few days when she just couldn't do it. On those days, I had an old hood from a Saab, and I used it like a sledge to haul supplies and firewood. I tied a rope to the catch in front, turned it upside down, and pulled on the rope.

It was one of those times, with a lot of snow, that I most remember. I had arrived from Fort NASDAQ the night before, and driven up the hill, as usual. But when I woke up the next morning, it was a different world. A foot of new snow had enveloped everything, sealing me in my steel cocoon. The world had been transformed, wrapped in its soft, white, cover, including the trees. I felt like I was 10 years old again, and school had been canceled for the day. As I looked out at the Honda, now entombed in its new wrapping, I realized it was likely canceled for a lot more than the day. I knew it would be impossible to leave. I would never be able to drive it down the hill now, and I didn't care. I had enough food and I was warm, so I enjoyed a couple of days of snowy bliss.

Then, the following afternoon, the muffled rumblings of some mechanical monster slowly became more and more audible. Finally, as I looked on in anticipation, Jack came into view, forcing his way up the hill, using the plow on the front of his Jeep. I was no longer stranded. I was grateful, but sad that my solitude was ending. It would be back to Fort NASDAQ the next day.

Summer

Eventually, winter did slowly recede from the top of the hill. At first, it was so brief that I did not even have time to actually get out my tools and get anything done. I probably enjoyed those days most. I could just let the earliest harbingers of spring that were flowing all around me flow into me. A warm day in March is like a miracle after the winter, just watching the snow melt. And it was nice to just fully experience that, and not be distracted from it by my dream.

As it got warmer and dryer, I could again continue work on the log walls. Wow, did that feel good! To be able to be outside, working again. Lifting something heavy. Feeling the burn, and the strength return. And watching my house and my body grow. The book cover photo was taken around this time.

But there was a problem. Mud. It was everywhere. And I was running out of logs. And at the mill? Forget about it. A muddy, mucky, moat most of the time, for weeks, months. I used every log I already had. The project slowed down.

And then, there was the black flies. They emerged in mid-April, and were present at least thru mid-May. They were at their meanest, hungriest from the last week in April and the first week in May. Clouds and clouds of the blood-sucking beasts. They were worst on cloudy, windless days, when they tried to eat any living flesh alive, consuming every drop of blood. Sunny, breezy days were much better, so that's when I got more work done.

I've been told that in Maine, they are fully capable, along with some help from the ticks, of killing a half ton moose, draining every gallon of blood from its body. Fortunately, Connecticut does have a shorter, and less intense black fly season. In Maine, it lasts most of the summer in the woods. But still, there were days when I elected to wear my insect net over my face, and of course, cover up all exposed skin, which did seem to slow them down a bit. Still, they were able to bite through a shirt.

Normal insect repellent does not at all impress black flies, who ignore it completely. But there is Skin So Soft. I think it is a beauty aid, and smells like an old lady's perfume. But they don't like it. I can't say I can blame them.

But there was another respite. Black flies are strange creatures. Unlike mosquitoes, they did not come inside the bus. In fact, they would not come under anything at all. It seemed to freak them out. Even a hat with a wide brim afforded some protection. And if you did not mind carrying around an unfurled umbrella, you could be safe.

Another thing: they are not active at night. I guess I could have continued my project on the night shift, but that did not appeal to me.

As spring slid into summer, the black flies diminished, and the buds on the trees swelled, morphing from red to green as they prepared for their rebirth. First it was the fiddlehead ferns, then the low brush, and finally everything opening, , up to the canopy of new, light green foliage.

Summer progressed, and so did the project. As the mill dried out, Gary, Henry, and I could resume cutting cabin logs again. With an adequate selection of logs to choose from, the log walls rose much faster, and the workmanship improved with practice. The project hummed along, in a sweet spot of reward and work.

I developed a rhythm that made the project swing. After my week at Fort NASDAQ, I loved Friday mornings, waking up in the bus, to the opera the birds performed. And not much later, it was Oliver the squirrel, screaming his head off, and pounding his tiny chest. It sure was good to be home again.

Then it was a quick breakfast of eggs scrambled right in the pan, toast, and coffee. I was eager to get to work.

I'm not a morning person, never have been, never will be. Still, I did enjoy getting out the chainsaw and maul, and cutting and pounding away the morning.

As eager as I was to get the work done, I always took an extended lunch break. Usually, it began with fabricating and eating two sandwiches at my outdoor, lumberjack dinette set. Then it was time for a much-needed rest. Often, I dozed off in my hammock, hung between two trees right behind the house site.

But if it was hot, I opted for a cooler lunch. Sometimes I took my lunch down to a spring fed stream below the hill. I liked to sit on a rounded rock in the middle of the stream, trying to dam it up with my naked butt, as the cold water sluiced away the sawdust and congealed sweat.

At other times, I drove about 20 minutes to a secret spot I knew about in the middle of the forest. It was the remains of a nineteenth century mill. A rather large stream was diverted through an iron pipe, three feet in diameter, and then fell into a pool deep enough to submerge into. I liked to grip the top edge of the pipe, and let the cold water levitate my body over the pool as it pushed against my chest and abdomen. Then I would let go, and fall into the pool. Cooled, cleaned, and rested, I was then ready to get back to work.

The afternoon was my favorite time to work. Finally, I was fully awake, both physically and mentally. I lost all track of time. Except for a short break for coffee around three, I was totally focused on the work. I worked hard, usually stopping around 5 or so.

After a short walk around the site, I was ready, ready, ready to eat, eat, eat. The kind of work I was doing does burn a lot of calories. I was always famished. Often, Hannah came to the rescue. She was an excellent cook, and completely understood the culinary needs of a hungry lumberjack. She had a full, functioning kitchen in the apartment she built over her cabinet shop, so that's usually where we ate. Sometimes, I made a meatloaf with baked potatoes in my outdoor kitchen and bought it down to share with her.

Around once a week or so, we went out to a local restaurant that served extra large portions. At other times, it was the local pizza house. I ordered one large, family size pizza and consumed it all myself. No danger of getting fat with the work I was doing.

The days were getting longer, and I had an adequate supply of logs to choose from. The progress accelerated, and the walls grew taller. It was tougher work, lifting the logs up there, and then having to work from scaffolding that I supported on the protruding ends of the logs. But I was getting stronger, and was developing more and more skill cutting the notches, so my craftsmanship improved. My pride grew along with my strength, and the height of the walls.

But it was a heavy load of work. I had expected that, had been warned about that. So, it was with some relief when Ella showed up. It was always the same. "You've been working too hard. Let's go to the beach." She already had a cooler of cranberry/orange juice, and we bought grinders on the way to Rhode Island, and a relaxing day at Moonstone Beach. Wow, what a break from all the hot, sweaty work, just lounging and looking at all the hot, sweaty bodies on the nude beach.

But it wasn't just the beach. It was incredibly nice, for a change, to get out of the woods, and be near the ocean. No bugs, cool breezes, blue and white instead of green. Ah, the beauty and joys of South County, Rhode Island. And then there was the self-service bakery, where you could pick up a loaf of freshly baked bread and leave your money in a can. A day at the beach was so much more than that.

Most of the time, I was up there on top of the hill alone,

and quite happy to be alone, focused on my dream. But at irregular intervals, I did get some help. Eugene helped set a row of logs up on the wall when he dropped by after school. He was an excellent driver of Jack's boom truck, and his work was essential as the walls rose higher.

I also got some unexpected help from friends from Fort NASDAQ. Alan came by early one morning, and gave me a full day of his labor, lifting logs, cleaning notches, and hammering spikes. He mentioned that it was hard work. At the time, that had not really occurred to me. After all, I was used to cutting firewood, moving rocks, digging, whatever. But of course, it is hard work. And I was grateful for his help.

And then there was the help I got from Thomas, my colleague from Fort NASDAQ. He and his girlfriend would come up on Saturday, and set up camp right on top of the hill. Initially, it was in a tent. But later, it was in a full-size house on wheels. I guess you would call it an RV. It had air conditioning, and a generator to power everything. Thomas would spend the days helping me with the logs, while she prepared gourmet meals. I appreciated the help, the food, and also the company.

The walls were getting towards the top, so I had to start thinking about what came next. First thing was to make sure all the log walls ended up the same height. The courses on the side walls were actually 3 inches shorter, half of a course height, than the front and back. So, we had to cut some special cabin logs 3 inches thick.

And then there was the second floor. I wanted the actual floor to be the ceiling of the ground floor. I did not want to cover the ceiling with some kind of veneer, such as sheet rock. It would be rustic from below. And from above, I wanted the floor to be tight, no cracks. This would need to be professionally milled, kiln dried, tongue and groove material.

My knowledgeable, helpful lumberyard came through again with a wonderful idea. They suggested buying a full unit of 6" spruce framing lumber, kiln dried. I could select out the best pieces to be sent to their mill to have them tongue and grooved, to be used for the floor planks.

The rest could be used to frame the upstairs gable end walls. Of course, I could have built them out of logs, instead of building a conventional framed wall. But logs are heavy, and the thought of having to lift them that high was daunting. How could I even do that? It was beyond the range of the boom-truck. And I was getting tired. The gable end walls would be frame construction, instead.

That's how I found myself one early August morning, astride a big pile of 2" X 6"s, flipping them into piles. It was spruce, cut in Maine, and I was very impressed with the quality. There was more than enough 2" X 6"s for the floor and walls.

To support the floor, I could cut some of the oak top logs into 6" x 6" joists at Gary and Henry's mill. And I would support them on two 8" X 8" beams down the center of the house. There was a lot of planning for this part of the project: cutting half height cabin logs, cutting 6" X 6" joists, and 8" X 8" beams. And last but not least, posts for the "tower". The tower has a long, complicated, creation story. More on that in a bit.

The main part of the cabin is a 24-foot square, so I would need to support the second floor in the middle someplace. I could have gone with a 12-foot span, but I decided on three 8-foot spans instead. The house would be on an 8 foot by 8-foot grid, and the joists and beams would be 8 feet long, and not too heavy. I would need 4 posts in the middle of the house to support the second floor.

But that's not all those posts would have to do. I knew the house would be off the grid, and relying on photovoltaic panels for all its electricity. In those days, they were very expensive. I would need to reduce energy use any way I could.

One important way to do that was to have water storage tanks above the second floor, in the house. That way, I could pump enough water for several days when the sun was out. On cloudy days, I would use water from the tanks. But water is heavy, so it would be essential to have a strong infrastructure to support the tanks. I over did it, and decided to use four 8" X 8" posts, to go all the way up through the first and second floors, to the water tank platform above. They needed to be 16 feet long, and turned out to be monsters. I hired Jack to haul the logs, and then the cut posts, on his flatbed truck.

The construction flowed smoothly as summer mellowed into fall. The walls were finished and the joists and beams were mostly on site. The flooring would be ready soon, and the lumber yard would deliver it.

It was time to take a deep breath, and look at what I had created. The walls were finished. Now, it was a log cabin. It still needed two floors and a roof, but it was a foundation and walls. I was probably more than half way done with my dream. I was filled with pride, but also relieved that the walls were done. Now the rest of the project would go much faster.

Finally, the huge 16-foot posts arrived, and were dumped into the yard, and there they laid. That was the problem. It was the next step, the first step of building the second floor. Each one would sit on one of the four concrete piers in the middle of the house's foundation. And then they would need to be stood up on end, and made perfectly plumb. And they weighed close to 350 pounds each, far more than I could handle myself. Someone would need to drive the boom truck, and I would want at least two helpers to do the job safely. But everyone was busy.

The project languished. Again.

Gloria

The project had stalled, but not Gloria. Hurricane Gloria. Once she crossed over the Outer Banks, she was pretty determinedly heading north. But where, exactly? Still too early to tell.

At first, it looked like she was heading straight for the island of Martha's Vineyard, where Hannah was in the middle of a house painting job. Hannah was preparing to hunker down, unhappy about the delay in her paint job.

But it soon became apparent that the path would have first landfall over Long Island, and then Connecticut. Oh great, so now a hurricane. What should I do to prepare? The log walls were up, but a little shaky. The sill seal between them gave them some flexibility, so I could get them to rock back and forth when I shoved against them near the top. There was no second floor pressing down on them to stabilize them. But it was hard to imagine that they would topple over. Those 10-inch spikes every couple of feet would certainly prevent that. Things were much more stable than if it had been a frame structure, with walls and no roof.

I didn't have any windows to tape up, or doors to secure.

All I had was holes where they would be, so that would just let the wind through. It seems there was not much I could do to get ready, other than bringing in my tools, and protecting the generator. Of course, I knew that my phone line through the trees would be toast, but I couldn't do anything to mitigate that.

In the midst of my non-preparations, the lumberyard called to say that all of my lumber for the second floor, including the tongue and groove flooring, was ready. When could they deliver it? After giving it a microsecond of thought, I said "After the hurricane." I wanted them to shoulder the responsibility if something happened.

But they convinced me not to wait. They were familiar with my half mile long bank-run gravel driveway, and pointed out that with the several inches of rain predicted, it might become impassable. I had to admit, they had a point. We scheduled the delivery.

As promised, the entire load was bundled tightly together with strong metal straps. I set up some log ends on the ground for skids, and they dropped the load on them, right up close to the east wall of the cabin. At least it would help to break the wind from that side, which was the most likely direction of the strongest winds.

That evening, as I walked around, surveying the site, I was a little tense. I decided to light up a joint, as I sat in the east door opening. It was the calm before the storm, but I was fine. Things were in a relatively stable place. It was not like I was in the middle of building the roof. I slept OK in the bus that night.

Next morning, I got up early and listened to the predictions. It looked like it would be a category 1 or 2, and come into the state in the midafternoon. They were advising anyone who lived in a mobile home to evacuate. Well, my home did have wheels, so it definitely fit that criterion. I decided I would spend the day in Hannah's shop at the bottom of the hill, away from the strongest winds.

I called Hannah to give her the latest. She intended to stay put on the Vineyard, and asked me to try to get Orville, her pet peacock, into the shop before the hurricane. Well, I'd never worked with birds before, so I had my doubts. I still don't know how I did it, but somehow, I got him into Hannah's shop. I set up a perch for him above the water tank in the corner, and he seemed to settle down there after a bit. I think he liked the novelty of being inside, since he was not normally permitted in there.

I turned on the TV to watch the approaching storm. It was moving quickly and crossed Long Island and the sound in less than an hour. Landfall in Connecticut was predicted to be around Bridgeport, which would put us east of the center, in the path of the strongest winds. So, I waited.

As it got windier, Orville needed to relieve himself by dropping his sticky, white, globs on the water tank, as he suspiciously eyed the swaying trees through the window. Soon after that, the TV died when the power went out. I turned on my battery radio.

Then the trees suddenly started falling all around us. The wind whistled, but the rain was less than I expected. There was a loud thump as a tree came down against the wall with the door. I could see that it had gotten itself tangled up in the power lines.

And then, suddenly, it was over. What was left of the very disorganized eye was over us. I wanted to get a quick look around outside before the wind came from the other direction. I tried to open the door, but it was blocked by the tree. I pushed hard, and got the door open wide enough to sneak through. Just then, Orville came flying, as well as peacocks can, across the shop and smashed through the partially opened door. I tried to get him back, but he would have none of it. It was all too crazy for him. I was concerned that he would be killed when the winds came from the other side, but there was no getting him back.

I sneaked through, and looked around. Wow, I sure was going to need my chainsaw. So many trees were down, I could count maybe 15 that I could see just standing there. The driveway was buried under wood, woven with downed wires.

It was only a category 1 or 2, but we were in the middle of the woods, or had been, before the storm. It was different now.

The wind from the other direction never happened. The storm was disintegrating, and moving quickly north. Soon, I knew it was safe to head to the top of the hill. I had to crawl through a maze of downed trees much of the way.

When I got to the construction site, everything looked fine. It was a clearing, and no trees fell across it. I looked over at the door opening where I had lit up the night before, and was astonished. There, sitting on the log at the bottom, was a flimsy, light, paper pack of matches that I had used to light up. How could it be? All those trees blown over, yet the light pack of matches sat on the log out in the open, right where I had left them. Weird.

I walked over to the bus. It was still there, but a tree had fallen near it, crushing the stove pipe that came out of the window. If I had been in the bus, I would be dead. Not from the tree, just the heart attack that probably would have killed me when it fell. My outdoor kitchen was a little disorganized, but mostly all still there. I would be fine. I moved back into the bus, and slept well that night.

Next morning, as I was sipping a cup of coffee in my outdoor dining room after tidying up, I had quite a surprise. A short, stocky, slightly brutish man emerged from the woods, carrying a shovel and a rope. And that was not all. Tattooed across his forehead, in large letters was "RIDER".

After the shock of seeing what the storm has blown in died down a bit, I offered him a cup of coffee, which he gratefully accepted. We proceeded to make small talk. But then, I asked him why he was carrying the rope. He said it was for his dog, who was missing. He asked if I had seen his dog, a bulldog, of course. I apologized but said sorry, I hadn't noticed a dog blowing on through.

I said that I noticed he was carrying a shovel, and by the way, what was that for? He said rather matter-of-factly, that he was looking for a cave, and thought the shovel might be of some help.

"So, why are you looking for a cave," I asked. His reply, "To live in."

I had to mull all of that over in my somewhat confused mind. The man, the dog, the cave, the hurricane. And "RIDER"? But I thought that it was just too personal to ask about that. I had nothing against the guy, hell, I hardly knew him. But still, it seemed best to put some distance between us.

"I think your best bet for finding a cave would be in the state forest over there," I volunteered. I knew the state forest well, and knew that there were several areas of large rock outcrops that no doubt had afforded shelter to many others over the millennia. I pointed to the trail, and was somewhat relieved when he disappeared into the woods. I did not think I would ever see him again.

I was wrong. Rider became my nearest neighbor. He set up camp on a beautiful ridge. His campfire was on top, where he had a nice view. And for the evening, he'd shelter under the overhanging rock just below. Often, I could smell the smoke from his fire.

Occasionally, I would drop by his campsite, sometimes sharing dinner with him. He subsisted on hot dogs and poached fish. The hot dogs came from Xtra Mart, and sold for 3 for a dollar. You could load them up with as much free condiments as the little cardboard tray could hold. They also became a staple of my diet in those days.

The "poached" fish was not cooked in water, just stolen from a neighbor's pond.

Rider was there through the fall, but as the winter set in and it got colder, he disappeared as suddenly as he had appeared. I missed my nearest neighbor. Years later, I came across pictures of the forest taken from the air. It was stunning, how isolated I was up there back then. It had been nice having another savage living with me in the jungle.

Gloria certainly had complicated my plans. Now, besides the stalled construction, I had a monumental cleanup project. Just clearing the tangle of downed trees off my half mile driveway was a significant addition to my "to do" list. Once that was done, I was able to get my generator down to Hannah's shop. Her freezer was loaded with food and it was obvious there would be no commercial electricity for a long time. It turned out to be the longest power outage in Connecticut's history, to that point, more than two weeks for us. But I was able to keep her freezer running a few hours a day, which was enough. And I could run Hannah's water pump, so at least we had water.

Eventually, the neighbors crawled out from under their downed trees, and dropped by to see if I had survived. Then they saw those four 8" X 8" X 16' posts sitting on the ground, just waiting to be set up. Only problem, I had not had enough help to do that.

Well, as usually happens at times like this, generosity abounds. They all had time to help. Without electricity, they had no work, but they did have time. And so, what Gloria taketh, Gloria giveth.

We raised those four posts together, and it took less than an hour to set and brace them. And I was able to offer something no one had had for several days: a hot shower. With Hannah's pump, my generator, and her propane water heater, we all luxuriated in hot showers. Then it was time to feast on all the food that was thawing everywhere. One generous neighbor even brought some excellent wine.

We were all showered, well fed, and happy to be alive. Against all expectations, the project was suddenly on track again.

Second Floor

So finally, I was finished with the log portion of the construction, and ready to embark on a new phase, the second floor. It would also be the ceiling of the first floor. Because of my "no vaneer-eal disease" pledge, the structural elements that supported it would be visible, and not covered by sheet rock, which is basically cardboard. They would get to show off their grain and strength. The spruce tongue and groove flooring would not be some flimsy chipboard covered with wall-to-wall carpeting. No, the planks were 1 1/2 inches thick and kiln dried, so there would be no cracks once they were anchored in place. From below, you would see the beautiful 6" X 6" oak joists every 3 feet on center. And in the middle of the house, those joists would be supported by the massive the 8" X 8" beams, which in turn would be supported by those big 8" X 8" posts we erected together after Gloria. This house would be massively over-built, according to the building inspector. That was fine by me.

But there was a problem I had to solve, and no one could give me definitive advice about it. When wood dries out, the fibers get closer together, so the log actually shrinks in diameter. It does not, however, get shorter. The amount of shrinking depends on the species of wood, the water content when it is cut, the length of time since it was cut, and the temperature and humidity around it. Basically everything. So, according to my rough calculations, the log walls could shrink up to 6 inches, or maybe not at all.

One end of the joists would be resting on top of the log walls, which were probably going to shrink. The other end would be supported by those big posts in the center of the house, which would not get shorter. If I did not account for the shrinkage, the second floor might be 6 inches higher in the middle than at the edges. I did not want to roll out of bed in the middle of the night, or develop skeletal issues from always walking on a slant.

I came up with a Rube Goldberg solution. I would not attach the 8" X 8" beams that supported the joists to the posts at all. Instead, I would let them rest on blocks that were attached to the posts. And in order to allow for shrinkage over time, I used 6 inches worth of shim blocks under each beam, resting on top of big blocks firmly attached to the posts.

It was quite a contraption. The big blocks that were attached to the posts were actually two-foot-long sections of 8" X 8" beams. They were attached to the posts with three big ¾" threaded rods that ran through a block, then the post, and then the block on the other side. It looked like I was building a bridge, and it probably was strong enough to support my ¾ ton pickup.

On top of each block was an 8" X 8" piece of ¼" steel. And above the edge furthest from the post, I had two pieces of ¾" rod that were drilled into the bottom of the beam that was being supported above. By tightening or loosening nuts on each rod, I could raise or lower the beam. It was like a built-in jack stand.

When it was time to lower the beams, I would first tighten nuts on the threaded rod, raising the floor slightly. Then, I would be able to remove the appropriate amount of shim blocks, and lower the floor back down on top of them. Voilà a level floor, I hoped.

It did work. Over the years, I had to lower the floor about three inches to keep things level. It would have been quite a crooked house if I had not done that.

Now that I had figured out how, it was time to build it. First step was to get those big 8" X 8" beams in place. I temporarily nailed 2" X 6" planks between the east/west walls and the posts. Then I used the boom truck to place the beams on top of the 2" X 6"s on top of the walls. Next, I used a rope to slide them across to the posts. After I got them in place, I used my built-in jack stands to level everything.

I needed to secure the beams in place, but still allow them to move down the posts as I removed shims. To do this, I attached 1/4" steel plates, one on each side, to connect the two beams on opposite sides of each post. I lag bolted the plates to the beams, but not to the posts. With the steel connector plates, it looked like the steel frame for a skyscraper, but with wood beams instead of steel.

Once the beams were in place, it was time to install the 6" X 6" joists. I placed them, one at a time, on the front or back wall using the boom truck. Then I attached a rope and pulled the joist into position from the opposite wall. I toenailed the joists to the beams, and spiked the opposite ends to the wall using 10" spikes.

The future roof rafters would be trying to push the walls apart. To resist this, I had been advised by an engineer to install sheet metal plates on either side of the joists, to tie them together. Each plate had numerous holes, so many fairly short nails where used. The joists were bonded tightly together and to the walls, but could still be raised or lowered if need be.

So, there it was. All of the joists and beams were installed in a few days. It felt great to be able to walk across the frame, 10 feet above the ground. The project was now moving along at supersonic speed.

The next step was to install the decking. I had been looking forward to this for two years. Finally, I would no longer be using a chainsaw, but just a portable skill saw. And I could easily do the work by myself.

Because this floor would not be covered, it would be the finish floor, and I did not want any nails to be visible. I decided to use a technique called "blind nailing". I nailed through the tongue, so that the head was set down into the tongue. The groove of the next plank would fit tightly around the tongue, which would hold it tight to the joist, as well as hiding the nail head.

I didn't want any cracks between the planks. In order to get a nice tight fit, I cut a wedge from a piece of material with a groove. Before I nailed down each plank, I placed the groove of the wedge into the planks tongue, and then hammered the wedge against a temporary block nailed to the joist ahead of the plank. The wedge forced the plank tightly against the previous one. Then I nailed it down through the tongue. Multiple copies of this arrangement on adjacent joists allowed the whole floor to be very tight.

Building the floor was one of the most rewarding parts of the project. This was so much easier than working with the heavy logs. It was fall, and the forest was in full color. I stopped frequently to look out from my 10-foot-high perch. The sharp air was infused with spruce fragrance as I cut each plank. The work was not particularly taxing, and the quick progress was gratifying. The floor was finished in a couple of days.

It was great to walk around up there, to imagine what it would feel like when that was my bedroom, looking out from the top of the hill.

But the second floor needed more than just a floor. It needed walls, but only minimal ones. My bedroom would be nestled beneath the roof, rising one foot for every foot across the house, a 12 in 12 pitch. I did not need any sidewalls, only walls on the gable ends: one on the south (front) side; one on the north (back) side; and one under the gable of the roof over the sunroom (east).

The walls would be conventional frame construction. The frame would be of 2" X 6" spruce, the same material as the floor. There would be a door and two windows on the south side to admit plenty of sun. The north gable would have two small windows to view the forest on that side. And the east wall would have a single, diamond shaped window to wake me up, when the rising sun pierced through there.

Conventional frame construction is a joy to build. The many pieces are lightweight: no heavy lifting. The lumber is dimensioned, so it is all of a consistent width and thickness. The window and door openings are easy to frame out. And because my steep roof formed a 90° angle at the peak, it was easy to lay out. I built each of the three walls laying down on the floor, nailing the framing together.

The walls were covered on the outside with plywood sheathing. I installed that while the walls were laying down. I think it only took a day and a half or so to build all of the walls.

At this point, you might be wondering what I would do to the inside of the walls, given my no veneer pledge. True, the spruce framing was pretty nice to look at, although the best ones had been used in the floor. And the back of the plywood, with its unfilled knot holes, was not so nice. And what about insulation? I did not want to be cold.

So, I cheated. I decided that I would break my pledge for the second floor. I was exhausted. I really needed a simple way to get the project finished. The bus was nice, but I really wanted the project to be moving along. And frame construction is so fast, so easy. So, I would cover the inside of the walls with, gasp, sheetrock. Basically cardboard. It would have been nice to use pine paneling, but I could not afford that.

Though it is true that there is no heavy lifting building the walls, there certainly is heavy lifting when it is time to raise them into place. I hired Jack to help me with this part of the work. It only took a couple of hours. There was one death defying stunt needed for the east wall over the sunroom, since there was no floor over that portion of the house. We nailed some temporary 2" X 6"s between the log wall below and the second floor. Then it was my turn to step out over the abyss, while we slid and then raised the wall. As you might have guessed, I did survive.

It felt good to look through the bedroom "windows" for the first time, but I was getting antsy. It was getting cold. Winter was coming. Any minute. Sooner than I expected.

Roof

The upstairs walls were standing, barely. They were propped up and braced with temporary supports going every which way. The wind was getting ferocious, and it was getting cold. Time to tie it all together and get a roof on. I hired Jack to help.

We started out by raising a ridge board across the full depth of the house, from the top of the front gable end wall to the top of the back gable end wall. It was a spruce, kiln dried 2" X 8", the same size that the rafters would be, and extended out over the front and back to support a future overhang. It was marked with the positions of the future rafters, on 24-inch centers. We held it up 12 feet above the floor with temporary posts. I looked forward to the next day, when we would start putting up the rafters. And then...

Freezing rain. The worst kind. It formed a smooth skating rink on the second floor. All of those joints I had struggled to be sure where tight worked, and managed to trap the rain completely. It was treacherous just to stand up there. And windy. And cold. But we endured. We managed to chip some of the ice away so we could stand up. And as we began to cut the rafters, we found that the sawdust we were generating gave us some traction, as it bit into the ice.

Most of the rafters over the main part of the house where fairly easy, if you discount the ice. But there were mishaps. We dropped the pointy end of one onto the floor, and it pierced the ice, and made a permanent nick in the floor. I was distraught at the time, but now that nick is a permanent reminder of what we went through to build the roof. It actually gives me some comfort.

We cut out a "bird's mouth" at the bottom, where each rafter would be nailed to the log wall. After we chopped away the ice on top of the wall, we were able to toe-nail the rafters to the wall. Later, I nailed hurricane clips to each rafter, to bond them to the log wall. We installed the rafters alternately on each side. Fairly soon, it began to be self-supporting, and I was actually able to hang on to the ridge board for support, instead of having to steady it as we added rafters.

But there was the issue of the sunroom. Its roof would intersect the main roof of the house. But because the span of its rafters was only 8 feet instead of 12 feet, it would intersect the main roof down below the main roof's peak. The sensible, easy, way to do that would be to let the main roof rafters be normal full length, and then simply let the sunroom roof rest against the main house roof. But no, that would be too easy.

I wanted the intersection of the two roofs to be open, so I could sit in my future office and look down into the sunroom. I also wanted the rising sun to penetrate into the bedroom through the window in the eastern gable end wall. I fretted for a year before the construction started, trying to figure out how to accomplish that. On a trip to visit a friend in Key West, I was overjoyed to find exactly my roof intersection in the attic of an old house. I took copious notes and measurements. Then when I got home, I even tried building a small model. It did not go well, but at least it did give me a preview of some of the things that could go wrong.

I honestly don't remember how we pulled it off. Maybe it was hypothermia. But somehow, we did frame that intersection, and it was strong. It looked great from both inside and outside the house. I'm still glad we did it, every time the light from that east window lights up the bedroom when the sun comes up.

There was one more complicated part of the roof framing to solve: the overhangs. In particular, the overhang on the south side was very important. The house would be oriented to the south to admit sun during the winter. But it was important to prevent that sun from blasting through the door and windows on the south side of the second floor in the summer. A large overhang above the door was needed. A roof overhang of around 3 1/2 feet would do it. Unfortunately, a roof overhang this size would block some of the winter sun from entering through the first-floor windows away from the center, since the roof there would be much closer to them. The solution was to have the roof overhang vary, from a maximum at the peak to its minimum at the eaves. This would also give the house the appearance of leaping forward toward the sun, a look that a sun worshiper like me preferred.

In order to support such a large roof overhang, I would rely on a "rake" construction. At 24-inch intervals along the rafters closest to the south wall, a 2" X 8" was nailed perpendicular to the rafters, supported on top of the gable wall. Then, on the protruding ends, cut to appropriate lengths, I nailed an outside facia piece. This piece would support the outside of the overhang. It sure was tricky nailing that last piece out there, hanging upside down out over the edge of the roof, with the wind howling. But in the end, it was worth it. The summer sun was blocked, and the house looked like it was leaping forward.

I also wanted to block at least some of the later morning sun from entering through the east window, so I designed the same type of variable overhang for that side. Because that roof was lower and smaller, I proportioned the dimensions appropriately.

The north overhang was the easiest. With no sun to deal with there, it simply had to keep the rain off the wall, so it could have a constant overhang. I also did not want to make the house appear to be leaping in both directions. The constant overhang on the north side helped to emphasize the south pointing orientation.

So, I had a strong, stable roof frame. The next step would be to nail 4-inch boards across the rafters. The final roof was going to be covered with cedar shingles. The accepted way to install them for my 12" in 12" roof slope was to nail across the 4-inch boards that were spaced one inch a part. For each row of shingles, 5 inches would be exposed, with a 1-inch gap, followed by 4 inches of the board. That would allow the undersides of the shingles to dry out, prolonging their life. It's much better than installing them over a solid plywood deck, which would just make them rot faster. And it did work: I managed to get almost 30 years from that first wood roof.

But there was a problem: I did not have the 4-inch boards. They would need to be pine, and I did not have pine on the land. And besides, Gary and Henry were not operating. Jack came to the rescue. He was able to procure the boards from a local saw mill in Massachusetts, and he would truck them down for me. Soon.

Well, actually later rather than sooner. But not much before Christmas, he labored up to the top of the hill, pulling a trailer loaded with all the 4-inch boards I would need. But there was, of course, a problem. Another ice storm. Snot, he called it, freezing snot. It did describe the texture of that stuff. It's not exactly ice, not snow, not rain. It's snot.

When we tried to unload it, we discovered what an excellent glue freezing snot is. We had to chip them apart in groups of 4 or 5, which seemed to be bonded together for life. It was like the bricks all over again, except in winter. I stood them up against the south wall of the house, hoping for a thaw.

Finally, a thaw, on New Year's Day. All the snot sloughed off. I stacked them, and of course covered them. The thaw also melted the ice off the second floor. Things were looking up.

Installing the boards was a snap. I snapped chalk lines across the rafters at periodic intervals. Once I got the first board across the bottom of the roof, I used some L-shaped jigs I made to space them 1 inch apart. Then it was just nail, nail,

nail. When I got up higher than I could reach from the floor, I found I could cling to the installed boards by inserting the front of my boot soles between them. I nailed temporary scabs on the finished part to make it a little less dangerous.

So now I had 4/5 of a roof. It certainly was not waterproof, with a 1-inch gap every 5 inches. And covering the roof with cedar shingles would be a time-consuming task. And then, how would I pay for the expensive shingles? I needed a temporary covering.

The solution was inexpensive building paper, 15 pound felt. It is asphalt-soaked paper, and is usually used as an underlayment beneath asphalt shingles. I would be living, at least for a while, in a tar paper shack.

It was to be a simple matter to unroll the paper, starting at the bottom, and staple it to the boards. Each successive layer overlapped the layer below. Temporary cleats were nailed on the lower course to provide some footing.

Well, it turned out to be not as simple as expected. The roaring January wind at the top of the hill tried to rip it off as we unrolled the paper. And there was nothing to hang onto once we got toward the top. I will be forever grateful to Cousin Bob who helped me one cold, dark evening, even after the sun went down, fumbling in the dark, trying to see the invisible black paper. We finished the job as the moon rose above the hill, trying to illuminate the dark paper.

So now I had a roof to keep the rain off my fine, finished second floor, and my head. Hannah came up one day, and installed plastic sheeting over all the door and window openings. So, in theory, I now had a house.

Well, at least the second floor. There was still no first floor, just dirt with the wind howling under the log walls. So, in theory, I could move in, but how would I heat it? I could move the small stove from the bus up to the second floor, but then I would need to carry all of the wood up a ladder. And there was no insulation. And so on.

I was exhausted. I really, really needed a break. And I needed some money. I was already comfortable living in the bus, so that's what I decided to do, through the winter. At least the house was now protected from the rain and snow. Finally, I could take a break and relax. And make some money at Fort NASDAQ.

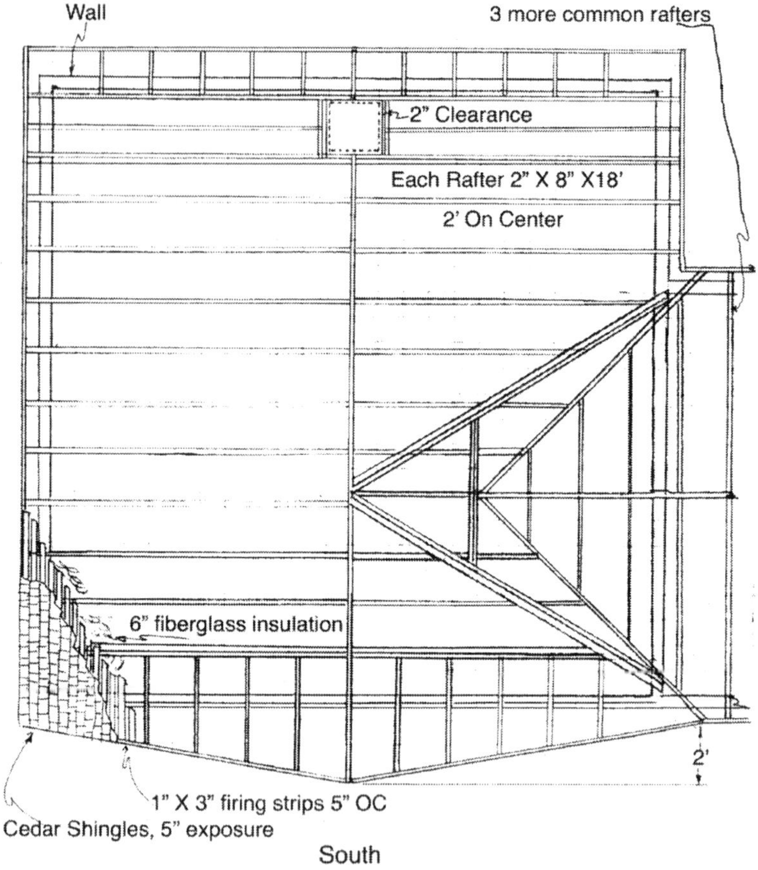

Roof Details, Top

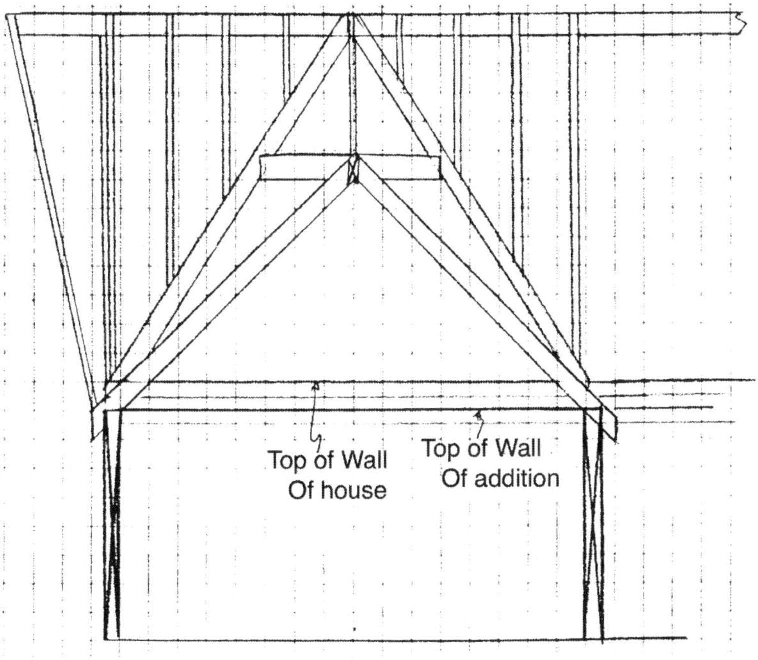

Roof Framing, East View

First Floor

Before I knew it, it was March. The days were longer, the sun warmer, and the sap was flowing, including my own. I was rested. It was time to get back to work.

So now I had a house, but it was actually an upside-down house. It had a tar paper roof, and a second floor, and walls around the first floor, but no first floor. It was just dirt, and the walls were raised up on their piers about 2 feet above the dirt. It was time to build the first floor. At least now, it would be a semi-indoor project protected from the rain, if you did not mind wind blowing through below. And where the black flies would fear to fly.

When I took the house building course at CHIF so many years earlier, I had asked them what would be the best use for the rough-cut native oak that I had. They said it would be best to use the oak for the floor joists. There would be no bounce in the floor, being supported by the oak. They were correct.

I had a stack of 2" X 8" oak joists that we had cut out at Gary and Henry's mill, stacked with small stickers in between to let them dry evenly. It was now time to use them. One end of each would be fitted into a slot that I had pre-cut into the second log row so long ago. The bottom edge rested on the first log course, which was directly on the piers. The other end of the joist rested on the 8" X 8" beams down the center of the house.

Most of the time, it was pretty simple. Drop each joist into the slot, and nail. But sometimes, the joist was too thick to fit in the slot, and I had to plane it thinner. And sometimes it was too wide, and I had to notch it on the underside. And sometimes it was too narrow and I had to shim it below. After all, this was not the dimensioned lumber from a lumber yard which would be planed to a uniform size. That would be too easy. No, this was rough cut, native lumbar. A 2" X 8" was "more or less" 2 inches by 8 inches. But it was far stronger than lumberyard lumber. And the cost was low.

Once the joists were in place, it was time to install the blocking. Blocking is composed of short pieces of 2" X 8" that are nailed between the joists to keep them from twisting. There was one row of blocking down the middle of the joists, and another on the end, above the beams. I wanted the blocking to be perfectly aligned so that the edges of the 4' X 8' sheets of plywood would always be above a joist or a block. That would prevent air from leaking through the floor. I found that I could nail one end of each block from the opposite side of the joist, and toenail the opposite end to the next joist. Other than nailing through the tough, dry oak, it was a piece of cake.

So now I had a beautiful grid framework of 4 foot by 16-inch cells. My friend Kevin came over, and we practiced walking on the top edge of it, without dangerously careening into each other. I would need that skill in order to complete the floor.

And now, for the very first time since the foundation, I had to begin working with something other than wood. It was time to install pipes and wiring. A log house is notoriously difficult to install plumbing and wiring. If you want wires or pipes in the walls, you need to install them while you are building the walls, but that was way beyond my capabilities. My plan was to run as much of that through the floor as I could. So it had to be installed now, before I put down the plywood.

The wiring was the easiest part. The outlets would be installed along the bottom perimeter of the walls, near the floor. That way, I just needed to run wires from each outlet under the floor to the circuit breaker box in one corner of the building.

The house would use solar electricity, and at that point I did not know if it would use standard 120-volt house current, or 12-volt recreational vehicle style appliances. So, I ran two cables from each outlet location, and installed two outlet boxes at each place. That would give me the maximum flexibility in the future. Belt and suspenders.

The downstairs would have only one interior wall, between the kitchen and future bathroom. I ran wires under the floor to come up inside that future wall. I also ran wires to where the island in the middle of the kitchen would be.

Wire runs across the joists were supported in holes drilled 6 inches from the top of the joists to protect them from nails from above or below. Wires run along the joists were stapled to the sides, also 6 inches from the top edge.

There would be very little plumbing in the floor because I knew it would be exposed to freezing. The only exception was a return line to the hot water solar panels, since I knew that it would contain a glycol solution to protect it from freezing. I pitched that pipe one quarter inch per foot, and surrounded it with cellulose insulation that I poured between the joists around it.

With the wiring and plumbing in place, it was time to install the insulation. I used sixteen-inch by five and a half inch thick fiberglass batts, 4 feet long. Each batt had paper tabs on the top that I stapled to the top of the joists. It went quickly, and miraculously, I never fell through.

Then it was time to install the plywood. I would be using cabinet grade 5/8 inch plywood that Hannah ordered for me. I nailed it down tightly using twisted flooring nails. The twisted nails would not pull up easily, so the floor would not squeak. All joints were above a joist or block. It was tight and strong. I could jump up-and-down on it, and my 203 pounds did not phase it at all.

The final step was to install 1-inch-thick Styrofoam insulation to the undersides of the joists. Since the 4-foot by 8-foot sheets were installed on the bottom of the joists, they prevented a thermal short circuit from developing, which would conduct heat through the joists. Wood is not a good conductor of heat, but Styrofoam would block any heat that managed to get through, keeping the floor warmer. It was a dirty job, crawling around under the floor. But it went quickly, with the large sheets.

So that was it. Now I had a first floor. It was starting to look like a real house. It was time to start moving in.

The very first thing I moved in was my brand-new propane refrigerator. The old, used Servell refrigerator I "purchased" from Hank with 5 loads of firewood never did work. It used ammonia instead of freon. Ammonia is incredibly corrosive, so the tubing was riddled with holes. And besides, who would I ever find to recharge it? But I knew I needed a propane refrigerator, because I knew my house would be running on very expensive solar panels, and I needed to minimize how many I would need. I bit the bullet, and ordered a new, expensive one.

When it arrived, I rolled it over to the northwest corner, which would become my temporary kitchen, and hooked it up to a small gas cylinder. It was protected, out of the weather, and the very first appliance in my new house. Wow, was it nice to have a refrigerator. Finally, I could eat ice cream whenever I wanted. And I no longer needed to rely on Hannah for ice. Really coming up in the world!

Bluefish

It was a midsummer evening, well after dark. A set of perfectly aimed headlights, one dimmer and flickering a bit, wove through the trees. It had to be Jack in his antique car with the six-volt electrical system.

"Hey John, want some bluefish?" he asked through the window as he pulled up. "Just caught at the Cape."

I love bluefish. "Is it on ice?" I inquired.

"Yeah, it's got ice on it," he replied.

We walked around to the back of the car, and he opened the trunk. A wave of Cape Cod washed over me: seaweed, mud, and fish. I shined my flashlight into the dark cavern, and it revealed a rather large heap of rather large bluefish on a bed of Boston Globes. And there, perched on top, were two or three small, mostly melted ice cubes.

I love bluefish. I wanted bluefish. But was it fresh? The flashlight glinted off the eyes, but the scales were dull.

"Sure Jack," I replied, somewhat apprehensively.

"Back your car around, and shine the headlights here," he directed.

Because of the somewhat primitive conditions, we decided

we would not attempt to fillet them. Instead, we would scale and gut them. So that's what we did, for an hour or so. Grab a fish from the pile. Hold it down by the tail on my cutting board, and then scrape the scales off, watching them sparkle in the headlight beam. Then slit them on the bottom from front to back, and scoop out the guts.

After a good rinse in my dishpan, I wrapped them whole in foil. The heads and tails would later be used to make fish chowder. Then I stacked them head to tail, filling most of the freezer compartment of my new propane refrigerator.

That fresh fish provided me with many satisfying feasts of high quality, delicious protein. My favorite was to place the whole fish on a broiling pan and fill the cavity with onions, herbs, and butter.

Every time I eat bluefish now, I think about that night, cleaning them in the headlight beam, and Jack's incredible generosity, taking care of me.

Chimney

Finally, finally, it was time to play with my bricks. It was time to build my chimney.

I always knew that my home would be heated with solar and wood. The solar was a no-brainer. Free energy? Why not. On sunny days in the winter, I wanted to capture as much heat as I could, through the large south facing windows. And it does work. My house is toasty warm on cold, sunny winter days. Most of my hot water comes from the solar panels in the front yard, but that is another story.

But the sun doesn't shine every day, so I would need to add heat. I wanted a fuel that was available nearby, and would not add fossil carbon to the atmosphere. It was all around me. I would be burning wood.

I planned to support two wood burning appliances. The first would be an antique, woodburning cookstove. It would provide sufficient heat in the spring and fall, and I could cook on it. The other would be a large heating stove, which could provide whatever BTUs I needed to be warm in the coldest months. Rarely would I need both stoves simultaneously.

The plan was to build a single chimney. It would contain

two thimbles, one for each stove. Of course, it would be brick, and lined with a clay flue tile in the middle. And of course, I would be using my antique bricks.

But before I could start, I would need to figure out where to put it. Exactly. My plan was to locate the chimney near the middle of the north wall, so that's where I put the foundation for it earlier. I knew it would be best to have it in the middle of the house, but I decided that that would put it really in the way. And since the first floor was mostly open, I knew there would be no problem for the heat to completely fill that space, no matter where the stove was. And of course, the chimney would be inside the house, to make use of all the heat it radiated.

I've seen old brick chimneys that twist and turn, but that was way beyond my capabilities. My chimney would be straight up and down, or at least that was my goal. I would need to thread it between the heavy floor joists of the second floor, and have it come out fairly close to the peak of the roof.

I made good use of my plumb bob. It's nothing more than a pointed weight hanging from a string. Gravity is pretty reliable that way. I wanted my chimney to be as straight as that string. I experimented with where the four corners of the chimney would be, starting just below the roof, inside the house. With the string tied up there, I was able to locate the hole in the second floor, and cut it out. Then I did the same for the first floor. I was very relieved that my chimney would be nicely positioned on the foundation I had poured two years earlier. I attached the four strings to the foundation by mortaring 4 nails below the first bricks. Now I had a nice guide to get the chimney all the way to the roof.

I started building the brick wall between the lines. I experimented with the joints between bricks until I got the rustic look that I wanted. Fairly quickly, I got the hang of it and had the walls up to the bottom of the ash pit, about 3 feet above the foundation. The bottom of the chimney below the ash pit was solid, so I filled it in with rock rubble and mortar. I built the cast iron door for the ash cleanout into the wall, and formed a concrete sleeve into the inside of the brick wall of the ash pit to support the flue tiles that would rest on it above.

I placed the first flue tile on top of the concrete sleeve, starting just above the cleanout door. I understood how important it was to get this first tile perfectly plumb. Otherwise, future tile would be leaning too much to fit in the center of the chimney. There is very little room to spare. Once the tile was in place, I built the brick wall around it, 7 bricks per course.

Soon, I was ready for the first thimble. Each thimble is a round clay pipe with an inside diameter of 6 inches. It is designed to conduct the hot flue gases from the stove through the brick wall, into the rectangular clay flue tile in the middle of the chimney.

You need to cut a big hole into the flue tile to accept the thimble, and it is as brittle as glass. How do you do that? I thought I knew. Wow was that a humbling, bumbling experience. I was armed with my carbide drill bit and a chisel. How hard could it be? Very hard, it turns out.

First attempt was to drill a ring of holes, maybe 2 inches apart, and then use the chisel to knock out the hole. Crack up the whole, was more like it. The entire tile shattered into three pieces.

Next attempt: put the holes closer together. That did seem to smoke the drill bit even faster. This time, a large piece of the tile broke away on the inside. Well, I quit for the day. I only had another two dozen flue tiles to play with, after all.

Third attempt went much better the next day, after getting some good advice. First, invest in a diamond tipped drill bit. Second, stand the flue tile up on a bed of sand, and then fill it with sand before working on it. Worked beautifully, my thimble fit nicely into the flue tile.

I continued the wall up around the thimble after chiseling some bricks to fit around it. Finally, I was at the top of the first tile. It was time to glue another one on top of the first tile. I learned just how important it was to be sure it was perfectly plumb if I wanted it to still be inside the chimney.

By the time I got up to the second thimble, just below the second floor, I was an "expert". No more smashed tiles. And the brick work went smoothly. I found that I could build about 2 flue tiles worth of height each day, around 4 feet. If I tried to go much higher, the chimney would sway. It was odd how I could push the thing side to side an inch or so. But not the next day, once the mortar had hardened.

Bricklaying was a meditative release of my anxieties. I just let it flow between the strings, plumb and level. Spread a layer of mortar on the wall. Grab a premoistened brick, put some mortar on the end, place it on the wall, adjust, and tamp down. Fill in the joint with mortar. Check level and plumb. Repeat. Repeat. Repeat.

After a while, the routine allowed my mind to wander. It had been almost 2 years since I moved into the bus. I had been very busy, both mind and body. But now, I had time to think about other things. Like my life.

My thoughts were interrupted by the unplanned arrival of a colleague from Fort NASDAQ. I was glad for his company. He looked at what I had accomplished, and said, "You must be very proud." That took me by surprise. I had not really been thinking about it that way. Sure, I had a great deal of satisfaction in what I had accomplished. But in a flash, I responded, "Yes but I'm lonely." I was feeling the ache of not being able to share my project with anyone. After he left, it was back to the bricks, and that eased the ache.

Mostly, the bricks are aligned pretty well on my chimney. But there are some that are tilted a bit, and those are the ones I cherish. I remember the help I got from my friend Bee, and how much fun we got from doing that together.

Before I knew it, it was time to cut the hole in the roof. Once I could crawl through the hole, I was able to get up on the roof to build the scaffold that I would need up there. It was more extensive than I expected. I needed space for bricks, mortar, and me up there. And don't forget, a flue tile or two. I attached 2 sets of 2" X 4"s at right angles, and set them gingerly on top of the building paper roof, like an acrobat doing a split.

Then I built a small platform on each side. I stretched the strings higher, and attached them to sticks nailed to the scaffold.

As you might expect, everything having to do with masonry work is heavy. Bricks, flue tiles, mortar, all heavy. Nothing like hauling all of that up above the roof of the house, and hoping that none of it, including me, also heavy, would fall off. I moved as much of it as possible through the hole in the roof, stacking the material on the scaffold.

Once the chimney filled the hole in the roof, I needed another way to avoid being trapped on the roof. Fortunately, I had considered this earlier, and set up my tall extension ladder against the roof of the house on the north side. But it was precarious, barely long enough, even sitting in the bed of my pickup truck. I sure was glad most of those heavy materials were already up there.

There was one more complicated thing to consider: flashing. I would need some way to close up the space between the brick and the roof, and it would need to be watertight. Not only that, it would need to deal with the fact that my house, like me, would grow shorter with age. But not my chimney. Bricks don't shrink, at least not after they're fired.

The solution I came up with was to embed the counter flashing into the brick work 6 inches above the roof peak, and let the future flashing be extra high. That way, the counter flashing sleeve I made would have plenty of coverage as the roof and flashing slid down. It has worked beautifully all these many years.

It didn't take long to get to the top. I let the last course extend out over the face of the chimney, to shed water. Then I capped the whole thing with concrete, and initialed and dated my work in the cap.

I didn't use the chimney right away. It had several weeks to cure before the first fire. But it did draw well. After all, it was 22 feet tall. And it has served me well all these years, warming my life when I really needed that.

Pig In a Poke

Well, building a house is an enjoyable project, but... Unfortunately, I did not have a generous benefactor that was meeting all of my financial needs. I needed to work for money to continue the project, and of course to eat.

There had been some significant changes at Fort NASDAQ. My consulting contract ended when the entire project I was working on was canceled. I was hired to patch up the existing brokerage network, but like an old car wheezing its last breaths, it was time to stop pretending it was the future, and just let it go. And me.

Sometimes in life, things just happen to work out. Fortunately, this was another of those times. About two weeks after my contract ended, I got a call from a colleague who was working on a new project at the fort, the Historical Database project. It was supposed to replace the old database with new technology. Apparently, management considered this would be a good idea after the magnetic drum the old system was based on came crashing through a cement block wall when its bearings seized. My colleague Alan had been hired to do the replacement, which would be based on new whizbang Digital

VAX technology. He needed help. I needed money. And so it went.

Now that I was working for Alan, there was a lot more flexibility. I could choose my own hours, and did not even have to record the time. I did, however, have to get the job done. It really is my preferred way to work. After all, if you don't get the job done, what's the point of putting in the hours? Just get it done. I did appreciate the increased flexibility. It made it easier to spend more time working and less time driving back and forth.

But freedom is not always what it's cracked up to be. So, I had the "freedom" to work on 4'th of July. And when I took my lunch walk, everyone around was relaxing, drinking, and barbecuing, but I had to go back to work. Wow, did I feel left out.

But it even meant I could "work from home". In those days, that was a new concept. But I did have an original 128K Macintosh computer, and a phone line running through the woods. Once I added a "fast" 2400 baud modem, I was good to go. I ran the computer and the modem on the bus battery using a small inverter. So "work from home" actually meant "work from bus", but who would ever expect that anyway. But it was painful. I could make small changes, but I did most of the work at Fort NASDAQ.

Initially, the project moved along smoothly. Alan had architected the whole thing, so all I had to do was build my share of the pieces, and make sure they worked. Most of the time, that was fine.

But there was a small wrinkle: Alan was getting married. This was not a spur of the moment thing. It had been planned long before. As often happens, the timing was not ideal. Alan and his beloved would be honeymooning on a Greek island, while I would be building my pieces. There were no phones on his island, thank God, and it was before the days of cell service. He had a wonderful honeymoon.

For the most part, my project went smoothly. Until, rather suddenly, I discovered that one piece needed access to data that it could not get to. And I had to get it working to meet the milestone. What to do?

After pondering the situation anxiously, I came up with a solution. If I substituted a different method for the search algorithm, I did not need access to the piece I could not get to. So, I built it, just to see if it would work.

It did work, at least with the test data I tried it on. My algorithm was simple and fairly fast, but I did not know if it would stand the test of time. And it was a fairly substantial change in the way the system worked.

Alan returned from his Greek island relaxed, radiant, and tanned. I was reluctant to tell him what I had done, so I let it go for our first get-together. But then my conscience began eating at me, so I told him.

At first, he did not really understand the magnitude of the change. But then, once he did, he said, "John, you've done a heart transplant on the system." That was essentially true. I sure hated bringing him back to reality that way.

He got right to work, testing, testing, testing. Finally, after a couple of pretty intense days, I got a call from him. He asked if I minded if he replaced my heart transplant with his. "Of course not," was my relieved reply. And so, he undid the open-heart surgery, changed the architecture, and got everything working again. We thought everything was fine.

It wasn't. The project was behind schedule. And it wasn't just us. The folks we worked with who were employees of the company and our previous colleagues also had their problems. The CEO was not pleased. He set up an early Monday morning meeting with all of us.

The night before was hot and sticky, and I was having difficulty sleeping in the bus. Then, soon after I fell asleep, an intense thunderstorm raked the top of the hill. The top of the hill does feel threatening at such times, and I was surrounded by trees, but sitting on rubber. I would be fine.

There was a snap and flash when lightning hit one of the trees supporting my stovepipe, and conducted its way into the bus, flashing me quite awake. I didn't get much sleep after that.

When the alarm went off in the pre-dawn darkness, I groggily pulled myself together and started out on my 2-hour drive. The plan was to meet Alan at a McDonald's near the fort to strategize. But when I walked in, I could see by the look on his face that something was terribly wrong.

He pointed toward my feet. "John, you're wearing two different shoes," he said in disappointment. He was correct. On my right foot was half a pair of dress shoes, and on the other foot, a single sneaker. Oh great, that ought to help me be relaxed and confident in the meeting with the CEO. I was horrified, but that was that. There was no time to do anything about it.

We drove over to the fort, and were led into the CEO's office, me first in line. He had a row of chairs set up for us all, in front of his desk. I quickly sat down when he did, and put my feet under his desk. And then the questions started.

He was going to get to the bottom of whatever had happened. There were questions for all around. And the answers, I was gratified to hear, were honest. As usually is the case, the blame is never on one side only. I guess he wasn't too happy with his people either. But he knew we were working very hard to get it done. It helped that one time when he dropped in on Alan at the fort, I was "working from home".

He looked us all in the eye, one by one. "Well, this sure is a pig in a poke, isn't it?" he said. He was not too happy with what his company had purchased. It wasn't a happy outcome, but then it wasn't all bad either. So, we bargained a bit. Alan and I got less money than we were supposed to get. And he got a working system, although it was late.

And finally, I got paid. So ended my career at Fort NASDAQ.

Water

Water, can't live without it. I always knew that I would need a well, and it was time now to start working on that problem. And quite an interesting problem it was, too.

My emerging house was located on top of the hill. That is usually not a likely place to find water. I knew it was quite likely there would be no water very close to the surface. But I also knew that I did not want to go very deep, either. My electricity would be coming from photovoltaic panels, and they were very expensive in 1985. So, my water problem was also a money problem, too.

Of course, I did not have a mortgage. But even if I had been able to acquire one, it is doubtful that the "unproven" solar panels would have been financed, even though solar panels had been successfully powering spacecraft for many years. Bottom line: I sure hoped there would be water fairly close to the surface, where it would not require too much energy to pump.

But what goes in, eventually comes out, too. Not only would I need a well, I would also need a sewage system. A roll of toilet paper on the handle of the shovel would not really be a permanent solution. Shit does tend to flow down-hill, and I was at the top of the hill. I did not want mine to be in my neighbors' wells down below. I had no argument with the state health district's rules regarding how my shit was handled. I would need an official septic system.

The septic system is, at first glance, pretty simple. A pipe would gather my drain and toilet water, and carry it into a tank by gravity. The tank would let the solids fall to the bottom, where bacteria would eventually eat them. There would be pipes closer to the top of the tank to collect the water now freed of the heavier solids. The exit water would be conducted to three rows of perforated pipes, where it would slowly leak into the surrounding material in a leach field. There, the water would evaporate, and any solids would be digested by bacteria in the material.

In order to protect the neighbors, the health department would be carefully monitoring the whole thing. Only a contractor licensed to build the system could be used. I had no argument with that. All I had to do was imagine myself building my house down below. I would not want someone else's shit in my well, that's for sure.

The first step in the process is a percolation test. A backhoe is brought in, and holes are dug in the area of the proposed leach field. Then, an engineer from the health department studies the material, and drops water into the holes. He carefully measures how long it takes the water to percolate into the surrounding soil. It must not be too fast, or too slow. The bacteria doing the work don't want to be drowned or die of thirst. Or have the effluent flow into the water table.

Since I had to pay to bring in the backhoe, I decided it would make sense to do an exploratory hole for a well. But when I contacted the contractor, I was informed that he would be glad to do the perc test holes. But if I wanted a hole for the well, I would first need to hire his dowser, so that he would know where to dig.

You may never have heard of a dowser, but many old-timers who grew up in the country have. Most scientists consider it pseudoscience, and believe it does not work. I was skeptical, but open-minded. Besides, I wanted to get the hole dug.

When I called Andy, the recommended dowser, he warned me that it would cost me $20, whether he found water or not. He told me he was donating the money to the Biafran Relief Fund. Biafra, a secessionist part of Nigeria, was having a terrible drought, and Andy wanted to help. It seemed like a win/win situation, so I invited him up to the top of the hill.

As soon as he emerged from his car, he looked around and said, "Oh, I think you have water here. Let's find out."

Then he got out his "equipment", a forked stick. As I remember, he said it was willow wood. He gripped it tightly in both hands, and started walking around.

Suddenly, the stick forcefully bent down, with the tip of the fork pointing to the ground. As he continued to walk, it released its pull downward. Slowly, back and forth he walked. Then he asked me to drive a stake into the ground at a specific spot. He said that was one point on the vein of water.

He continued marching back and forth across my front yard, noting where the stick pulled down. Finally, he asked me to drive a nail into the bottom log of the cabin, in a very specific place. He said that the vein went from that nail to the stake, and that the water was coming from behind the house, to the north.

Then he asked me if I wanted to try it. I accepted the challenge. He handed me his stick, and instructed me to hold onto it tightly, and walk around. So I did, blindly. And much to my surprise, the stick moved, and not feebly. It strongly pointed down, right over the vein. Of course, I already knew where the vein was.

A year later, I finally had enough money to have the well dug. The first 5 inches was topsoil, from decayed forest leaves. Then there was around 2 feet of subsoil, composed of sandy loam: a mixture of sand, stones, and clay. Below that was hardpan: a dense, impenetrable layer of mostly clay. And then, finally, a wet layer of sand and gravel, around 12 to 15 feet below the surface. The gravelly layer was about 4 feet thick, and below that, more hardpan. As the hole got wider, we could see that the gravel layer formed a "V", right where Andy said the vein was. And when the water started flowing into it, it came from the north, just as he predicted.

Years later, it occurred to me that there was a rocky area on the north side of the hill that had a seasonal spring on it. I now believe it is the source of my vein, which runs under the north side of the hill.

I still don't know how Andy did it. Was it possible he smelled the water? I know I've been able to smell water ahead on the Appalachian Trail, even one mile ahead. Maybe Andy is sensitive to things he is not aware of. Maybe it's the vagus nerve, somehow stimulated by the flowing water. Scientists have not been able to prove that dowsing works, but I believe it does with the right person, and I'm grateful.

So, after seeing the water in that original test hole, we set a vertical piece of perforated pipe back in the hole and back filled. I had hopes of being able to pump water out of that hole, but it was not very successful. The limited water was too contaminated with dirt. But the real well I had dug later in the same spot provided many years of clean, reliable water.

So much for the well. It was time to move the machine to the leach field. Those holes did not need to be nearly as deep. But they revealed exactly the same thing: 5 inches of topsoil, 2 feet of sandy loam, and then hard pan. They moved the machine out, and I awaited the engineer from the health department.

His test did not take too long. He filled the hole with water to a specific depth, and then timed it to see how long it would take to drain out. It never did. My soil had too much clay. It was impermeable. The verdict: I would need an engineered system.

My system would need to be a marvel of engineering. A new layer of fill, with the correct characteristics, would have to be trucked in and spread across the area. Then the perforated leach field pipes would need to be dug into that. The field would then be capped with a vapor permeable fabric that would keep rain water off, but let the leach water evaporate. The whole area had to be graded to keep rainwater from flooding the field, then the concrete septic tank would need to be buried at the correct grade. Finally, everything had to be hooked up with pipe. Bottom line: lots of money.

It was a good news/bad news situation. Yes, I had a reliable source of pure water close to the surface. But the septic system would eat a whole lot of money. At least now I knew what I was dealing with. Time to move on.

Doors and Windows

Wow, was I on a roll. I had gotten paid so I could start eating again. Now that I had money and time, with Fort NASDAQ finished, I could continue with the project. I already had a second and first floor. What could be better than that?

How about some doors? The plastic sheeting Hannah had installed a year earlier was still intact and stretched tightly across the window holes. But the door holes were just: holes.

Before I could do anything, I needed to install the oak splines into the notches in the ends of the logs around the door openings. I cut a 2" X 2" spline for each side. The length depended on clairvoyance. I did not know how much the house would shrink. Since I had not figured out how to predict the future, I had to guess. I wanted to be sure I left enough space above each spline so that as the logs shrank, they would not be held up by the spline. I left plenty of space at the top of the notches, and filled it with fiberglass, which would compress if need be.

Hammering the splines into the notches was not so easy. If there was a bit of mis-alignment of the logs, the spline would get hung up. It was an incremental process of some fine tuning with a chisel, and the force of the 7-pound mall that finally got the job done. But after the splines were hammered in, the walls were much more stable. This was especially important for the short wall segments of the south wall.

I liked the look of French doors, with their small panes of glass taking up most of the door. I love sunlight, and can never get enough. Since the doors were on the south side, they would admit a lot of sun in the winter. And in the summer, I could open them wide for plenty of fresh air. Many years before I started the project, I had acquired several old, interior French doors that were salvaged from an old house that was being renovated. I would use two of them together in the wide hole on the first-floor south side, one on the door hole on the east side, and one on the second floor.

A friend of mine who was a professional builder pointed out to me, with a touch of disdain, the obvious: the doors I intended to use were interior doors, and I was about to use them on an exterior wall. I'm sure any professional builder that tried to do that would have soon been unemployed. But it did work for me. The doors were under large overhangs, and almost never got wet. They lasted at least 20 years, until I finally replaced them years later with nice, thermopane doors. And in the meantime, I saved hundreds of dollars I did not have. The doors cost $20 each, and the lumber was 10 cents a board foot.

Though I had the doors, I had nothing to attach them to. I would have to build that. Fortunately, I had those oak boards that were cut from the original logs. They were rough-cut, and not planed smooth, so working with them was challenging. I would need to build the jambs to surround the doors, and anchor them to the splines in the grooves around the door openings. Extreme care was needed about plumb and level, or the doors would never close properly, or at all. Making door jambs, especially for double doors, especially with rough cut lumber, is not considered simple, and my carpentry skills had been honed with a chainsaw. As you might imagine, it did not go smoothly or quickly.

I started with the single door on the east wall, since I knew it would be easier than the double doors. To start, I cut an oak 2" X 8" plank to the door opening's width, to act as a door sill. Using my hand plane, I beveled the outside top edge slightly, so it would shed water. I cut a shallow grove with my skill saw in the bottom, outside edge to act as a drip edge. Next, I put shim shingles under it, as needed, to level the top surface, and aligned the inside edge with the inside of the wall. Then I nailed it down to the bottom of the opening, using ringed nails that would be impossible to remove, as I later discovered.

Next, I found two nice oak boards, 1" X 6", with few knots, to go on either side of the door. I cut them 1/2 inch longer than the door's height, to provide 1/8 inch above and below the door, and to protrude ¼ inch into a notch in the top jamb, which I would need to make.

I positioned one on the hinge side against the door, with the hinges on the inside edge. I marked the hinge positions on it, and chiseled out a thin slot for each of the three hinges, so that the new jamb was tight against the door. I screwed the hinges and door onto the new hinge jamb side.

Next, I temporarily propped up the door, with its hinges attached, near the opening, being sure to lift it off the sill 1/8 inch with some shingle shims. The non-hinge side was much simpler, with no notching required. I positioned it against the door, and propped it up as well.

To make the top jamb, I cut a nice piece of an oak board two inches longer than the width of the door. Then I cut a ¼ inch deep notch on each inside end, one inch wide. That was to accept the left and right jambs. The notch would prevent the weight of the door from causing the top jamb to move, maintaining the width of the opening. I nailed through the top jamb to attach it to the two side jambs.

The final step sounds simple, but it was not. I needed to attach the jamb to the splines. But I needed to be sure that the door jamb was completely square with the door and the door sill, and more or less plumb, while still mating with the existing wall. I knew that it was unlikely that the opening that I cut with the chainsaw was perfectly square. I positioned the door and jamb in the middle of the opening, and used my level to make sure the hinge jamb was as plumb as possible. Next, I used small blocks of wood and shim shingles to fill the gap between the jamb and the spline. I used 3 sets of blocks/shims, one behind each of the hinges. Then I temporarily nailed through the jamb, into the blocks and spline, with long nails. And voila, the door opened and closed. Or not. Some trial and error was needed.

The jamb on the other side was much simpler. I used the same block/shim method. I had to be careful to not crunch the door too tightly, or let the jamb be too far from the door. Again, trial and error.

The doors I had already came with the knobs, which were either old, gorgeous brass, or glass. I loved them. The opening and locking mechanisms were also already in the doors. All I needed to do was to cut a shallow notch into the jamb for the striker plate that I bought at the hardware store. Then I drilled holes for the latch bolt and dead bolt to fit into.

So far, so good. But there still was a rather big gap, at least in places, between the jamb and the splines and wall opening. To fill that, I custom ripped some oak boards to fit over the splines in the opening on the outside. I filled the gap on the inside with fiberglass insulation. Interior trim could wait till later.

The finishing touch was to install a foam weather stripping I bought at the hardware store to the outside of the door jamb. The door closed tightly up against it. I was good to go.

So that was the easiest one. Now for the double door. The method was basically the same, with some variation. The top jamb and sill would, of course, need to span both doors.

The two doors I had for the south opening were already a pair when they were salvaged from an old house. Though both doors could be opened, one was normally the fixed one, which would accept the latch and dead bolts, and the other, with the knob, was the one that would normally be opened first.

I made the two side jambs the same way I had made the hinge side jamb for the single door. I screwed each door to its respective side jamb. The top jamb was the same, except for its longer length to span both doors. I nailed it to the side jambs. And the same, for the sill.

I began the installation with the side jamb for the fixed door. I anchored it to the spline with blocks and shims, trying to make it as plumb and level as possible, while still letting its inside edge be flush with the inside of the wall.

Then I did the same for the door with the knob. Naturally, there was a lot of trial and error, and much adjusting, opening and closing the doors until they worked well. I found that the springiness of the jambs on either side helped the two doors mate tightly together when they were closed.

The final step was to add a sliding bolt to the top and bottom of the fixed door. I drilled a hole in the sill and top jamb for it to mate into. It held both doors securely closed. And then, the finishing touch, the weatherstripping on the outside.

After a week or so, I had working, closing, doors on the house. Over the years, I was quite impressed with how well my homemade un-pre-hung doors had performed. Years later, when I could afford the $2000 to $3000 cost for a double pre-hung door set, it was not any more stable in the log walls, which continued to shift around. Of course, the thermal performance of those doors was much better. But I found that I could place a 1" thick sheet of Styrofoam over my doors at night, and do even better that way.

Now that I had front doors, I needed to do something about a front porch. During the construction, I got by with a simple, 2" X 8" plank ramp, from the ground up to the first floor. It was ok, but not ideal. I remember one time when Ella dropped by with her grandmother, to show her the house. Grandma was very spry, but I did worry when she started up the ramp. But she easily cruised into the house.

I decided to make a simple front porch and steps. The porch was the 4' X 8' body of an old solar panel that had frozen and become useless. I propped it up on some pieces of firewood. Some big blocks cut from the ends of the 8" X 8" beams became my front steps. The house was becoming civilized.

So much for doors. What about windows? I was planning on having plenty of those. Before the construction started, my builder friend alerted me that a local building supply store was clearing out old inventory. They had a stash of old, single pane Anderson windows. He suggested making them an offer for the whole lot. Sounded good to me. Anderson windows had an excellent reputation. I would check it out.

It was quite a collection. There were a few pre-hung, awning style windows of various sizes. They had groves where a second pane of glass could be added, if I was so ambitious. And there was quite a stack of just window sash, not mounted in any jambs. I assumed I could use them, too. I made an offer of $200, and drove away with a truck load of windows. I made a storage area for them behind my outdoor kitchen, and covered them with a tarp.

Unlike with my bricks, at least I had specific plans for the windows. Before I started the log construction, I knew the dimensions of the awning windows I had, and made plans to use them for the three windows in the sunroom. And I would use some of the smaller, unmounted windows in the bathroom and north wall, where I would need to build jambs for them. I would use one of the tall, narrow windows in the west wall, to allow me to see the setting sun. And I would use two more of them on either side of the upstairs French door.

Originally, I had planned on the two big, south-facing windows being bay windows. I had enough of the fixed Anderson windows to do that, using 4 of them for each of the two holes. But as it got closer to the time to fill in those big holes, I had second thoughts. Bay windows do not do well from an energy standpoint. So much heat can flow out all around and above and below them.

As luck would have it, a friend showed up one day with 4 large windows with small panes in his truck. He had rescued them from the transfer station. They were very old but in good shape. The glass panes exhibited the effects of glass actually flowing over time, so they were thicker on the bottom than the top. I loved the slight distortion I got looking through them. And, of course, I respected their age, and what they had seen in their long lives. And, the clencher, they were exactly the right size to fit in the openings I already had. And they were free!

I made plans to use them. I decided they did not need to open. I knew I would already have a lot of ventilation through the three French doors downstairs. I would need to build jambs, but would not need any hardware. I used the same techniques I honed on the doors, but it was much easier because everything was fixed.

I also made jambs for the tall window on the west wall, and the 4 tall windows on the upstairs south wall. None of these needed to open, either. And the 3 windows in the sunroom already had jambs, so they were easy.

But truth be told, I did not have the energy or time to build jambs for all of the windows just then, especially the ones that needed to open. That did happen in good time. But in the mean-time, the plastic that Hannah had stretched over the openings did an amazing job of pretending to be windows. I lived with them for quite some time.

So, I had doors and windows.

Moving In

I had two floors, walls, and a roof over my head. I had a house. It was time to start moving in, something that I had been looking forward to for a long time.

To start off, I thought it made sense to move my kitchen and dining room. After all, the dining room was outdoors. Wouldn't it be nice to not have to dance around the rain drops, preparing and eating breakfast, lunch or dinner?

My new, expensive gas refrigerator was already in there, against the west wall, just waiting for company from the other appliances. I knew that it was not the place where the kitchen would permanently reside, but it was out of the way, and near a plastic window, where I could route a sink drain temporarily.

So, I moved my kitchen propane range in. I loaded it on the truck, and rolled it in, against the west wall. Finally, it was indoors, where it was meant to be. I would be able to rely on the baking times in the recipes, and not have to double the times because my stove was outdoors, in the cold and wind.

Next to the stove, I gave pride of place to the original hickory counter that I had struggled to build on my first day. I attached a magnetic knife rack to the side, just like in a real kitchen.

Hannah had given me a section of counter top with an embedded stainless-steel sink she had removed from a kitchen she was renovating. I set it up near the plastic window on the west side, and attached some pipe to its drain. I punched a hole through the plastic window, and had the pipe drain out not far from the house. It was only gray water, and the weeds out there seemed to be grateful for it as they slurped it up. I still did not have a water supply, so I placed the 2 1/2-gallon jugs I filled at Hannah's next to my new sink.

The final piece was to move my outdoor table, complete with tree stump legs and plank benches, into my new dining room, right next to the kitchen. As I surveyed my new indoor kitchen/dining room, trying to determine what style it was, Early American Lumberjack is what came to mind. It was nice being able to eat indoors in true luxury.

It was time to move the rest of my possessions into my new home. I had moved before several times in my life, but this would be different. I was moving into a home that I totally owned, debt free, for the first time in my life. And a home that I had built with my own hands, on my own land. It was my dream home!

But it was a different kind of move in a purely logistical sense, too. Instead of moving my possessions into the truck and hauling them to the new house, I simply hooked up a chain between the bus and my tractor, and towed my old home to my new home. I positioned the bus alongside the house, and set a plank between the bus and my front porch. It only took a few minutes to transfer everything I owned into my new home.

Moving into the upstairs bedroom was a little more complicated. I did not have stairs to get up there, only a hole in the floor with a ladder. I had to schlep the mattress up the ladder. And then I just set it on the floor, in the middle of the room. I would wake up to spectacular views of the surrounding forest. Later, I hung a mosquito net from the rafters, so I could sleep undisturbed by the bugs.

The final step was to tow the bus out of there. With a friend behind wheel, I towed it down the hill with the tractor. Then we pulled it not far off the driveway, into its resting place in the woods. Since it had been home to both Hannah and I, we positioned it along the border between our respective pieces of land.

I had to admit to just a bit of sadness, seeing the bus leave the top of the hill. After all, it had been my home, and a good home, too, for an important time of my life.

Later, Jack came to repatriate the cap he built that had been the roof of my outdoor kitchen. Once that was gone and the site was cleaned up, there was no trace of where I had lived for more than 2 years.

Home

At first, it was a little disconcerting, living in my new home. It's true that all of my Early Lumberjack furnishings were the same. But now, I had so much more space, and besides that, I could actually stand up! And then there were the wonderful views from the upstairs bedroom, on top of the house, on top of the hill. It didn't take too long to feel right at home.

But the earth was turning, and time was passing. It was starting to get cold. Again, Hannah came to the rescue. She loaned me her antique Warm Morning parlor stove. It was basically a steel cylinder, about a foot and a half in diameter and 2 feet tall. There was an ash cleanout on the bottom, below the grate. It had a hinged, cast-iron door on the top, near where the stove pipe came out. The stove's most appreciated feature was the amount of wood it could hold, and the size of wood you could drop in there. I would not need to split it small, and the load would last until morning, hence the name. It did work.

And the chimney? Wow, it drew beautifully. The 8" X 12" flue, and 22-foot-high chimney perfectly serviced the big, old, stove.

I decided I would temporarily relocate my bedroom to the first floor, near the big stove. I put together a simple bed platform of plywood, and located it in the northeast corner of the house, which would someday be the bathroom. Curiously, it was the same area that had first sheltered me so long ago, when I rested my back up against the log walls on that pristine fall day. Now, the logs, the stove, and the chimney did the same.

So, I was moved in. I had a warm, comfortable place to live. And it was mine, free and clear. I loved it. It was home.

But it was not finished. There was still so much to do. I had windows to install, a roof to finish, plumbing, electricity. But I was out of money again.

As it got colder, the coyote's howls grew louder. They had to eat, and so did I. At first, I was in denial. But eventually, I began to accept that I would need to find work again. And I knew it would not be around home. Not enough, at any rate, to finish the project.

I did not know where I would go or what I would do next. But I did know where I had been, and what I had done. I had created a dream, with my own two hands. And I had been at home, on the land, in the bus. The bus years had been the most difficult, the most creative, and the most intense years of my life. Years that I will cherish for the rest of my time.

The years I lived in the bus. And the years I built my dream.

Epilogue

So, you are probably wondering, what happened next? I, also, wondered about that for a while. I knew I needed money, so I knew I needed a job. The rural area where my dream was located, like many, was critically short on jobs, at least any that would simultaneously allow me to eat, and save enough to finish the dream. So, I knew that I had two basic choices. I could find a job within commuting distance, or be away from my dream during the week.

I do not enjoy spending time in the car, so I knew a long, daily commute would leave me miserable. Besides that, it would eat many hours of time that could be more profitably used by, for example, recovering from a busy weekend building my dream.

Fort NASDAQ had been great, because I had been able to score a 3-day weekend. I knew that it was unlikely I would be so fortunate again. So, I looked more widely afield.

Fortunately, there was Amtrak. Judicious use of it would allow me to access work in New York City, among other places. I had previously spent a couple of years living and working in New York. I very much enjoyed the city, and of course the money it allowed me to accrue. And I enjoyed the professional stimulation of the people I worked with. You know what they say, at least in New York. If you can make it in New York, you can make it anywhere. There is some truth to that.

How, you might ask, could anyone so tuned in to trees, squirrels, and nature tolerate New York City? Easy. I had a tree directly outside the window of my 6-foot by 12-foot room with a shared bathroom. The room was not as big as the bus. The bed only fit along one side. And the tree was nothing to write home about, but it was my home away from home for a while.

I found that I could be comfortable in the city, or comfortable in the country. But, where I do not enjoy being, is the suburbs. For me, they do not offer enough space, quiet, or nature to satisfy. And, the constant need of depending on a car doesn't work for me, either. I need to walk. The worst of both worlds.

So, it was a 2 ½ hour train ride on Monday morning, and another on Friday evening, followed by a 40-minute car ride. And very soon, my project was refunded, while I could eat falafel during the week.

The first step was the well and septic system. I had previously cleared the land, and the dowser had already located where the well would be. All I had to do was shell out the bucks, and now that was easy for me. It was gratifying to see it all come together so quickly.

I bought an old-fashioned hand pump, and positioned it on top of the 19-foot deep well. It had a lever on the side to route water through an underground pipe, into the house, and up into the 5 55-gallon tanks above the second floor. I found that it took 20 minutes of strenuous pumping on my old-fashioned rowing machine to provide a good aerobic workout, and enough water for two days use, including one flush/day.

The first flush was magical, as I listened to the water sloshing down the empty pipe, and cascading into the empty septic tank at the end. No more toilet paper on the shovel handle.

The next order of business was to complete the skin of the house: the windows, and the roof shingles. My new boyfriend

Oscar and I spent most of the next summer's weekends replacing Hannah's plastic windows with my Anderson home made windows. Then we went to work nailing the very expensive red cedar shingles, #1 perfections, over the spaced boards. That roof lasted nearly 30 years.

In 1992, I finally was ready for my electrical system. I purchased 12 35-watt used solar panels that had previously been in use in the Mohave Dessert. They had been part of an experimental system, and the builders of that did their best to destroy them by focusing a lot of sun onto them. The substrate was burned brown, but they kept going, and in fact are still producing 300 watts.

My initial battery bank was 12 6-volt lead-acid deep cycle batteries, like the kind used in fork lifts and golf carts. I did need to add water every 3 months or so, but they powered my home, in super-frugal mode, for 10 days without sun.

My initial water pump was a 12-volt Sure flow, like the kind that are used on boats as bilge pumps. It was a little noisy but worked great. In fact, as soon as I got it working, I abandoned my rowing-machine pump, never to use it again. I get enough exercise, anyway.

In the beginning, I used mostly 12-volt incandescent lighting, and some 12-volt fluorescent. But technology marched along quickly, so I got the benefit of LED lighting before vary long. And, as inverters got more capable and cheaper, I eventually abandoned most of my 12-volt circuits.

In later years, after a drought year when my dug well nearly went dry, I had a deep well drilled, with a submersible pump. The new inverter made that possible.

I kept adding solar panels. At this point, it is a total 1.6 kW system. My array looks like a museum of solar electricity, but those old modules are still cranking it out. I converted my battery bank to 16 batteries running at 24 volts. I am on my fourth set, and they have been lasting 10 years each. The lead-acid batteries are still much cheaper than lithium-ion, and they are recyclable. Recently, I replaced my propane refrigerator with a modern, efficient electric one.

The house, too, has been upgraded. In the early 2000's, my husband Jose and I hand built a timber frame addition on the west side. We cut the frame of the west wing ourselves, and installed stress-skin panels over the frame, so it is well insulated. Between the log cabin and the west wing, we built a masonry heater, which supplies almost all of our heat. After it gets up to operating temperature, it consumes all of its own smoke and creosote, and is very efficient.

Over the years, the outside also evolved. There is a large vegetable garden where we grow most of what we eat, along with venison harvested from the land. There are numerous fruit trees, and a ¼ acre grape vineyard. Later, we built a barn and workshop, with a wine cellar and winery in the basement.

What's next? Who knows? But it will, for sure keep evolving.

And being home.

The cabin in 2024 with West Wing and screened in porch

Acknowledgements

Most of all, I am grateful to Robert Solywoda, aka Cousin Bob, for his fantastic photos and editing, and help putting on the roof in horrendous conditions.

I want to thank Christine Acebo, for her photo of Jack, and for pointing out deficiencies in the original manuscript, which resulted in important changes that made this a much more honest book. Many of Christine's ideas strongly influenced the house design.

I am grateful for the help and encouragement of the late Robert Otten, without whom this book might not exist.

I will never forget the help, and encouragement of the late Carol Yee, who showed me the way.

I will always remember the many gifts of the late Ed Cruikshank, who taught me how to live in the woods, and so much more.

I appreciate the suggestions of all those readers who gave feedback on the manuscript.

Finally, I will be forever grateful for the help of all those who "stopped by" to visit that I put to work. They never complained, and their labor helped me build my dream.

Made in the USA
Columbia, SC
05 December 2024

48545625R00105